Hollywood's Gangster Icons: The Lives and Careers of
James Cagney, and Edward G. Robinson

By Charles River Editors

Humphrey Bogart and Lauren Bacall in *Dark Passage* (1947)

About Charles River Editors

Charles River Editors provides superior editing and original writing services across the digital publishing industry, with the expertise to create digital content for publishers across a vast range of subject matter. In addition to providing original digital content for third party publishers, we also republish civilization's greatest literary works, bringing them to new generations of readers via ebooks.

Sign up here to receive updates about free books as we publish them, and visit Our Kindle Author Page to browse today's free promotions and our most recently published Kindle titles.

Introduction

Humphrey Bogart (1899-1957)

"All you owe the public is a good performance." – Humphrey Bogart

Americans have always loved movie stars, and there have been no shortage of Hollywood icons, but one man has long been considered the greatest male star. From the time he first became a leading man, Humphrey Bogart's screen image has resonated with viewers more than perhaps any other actor. At the end of the 20th century, when the American Film Institute assembled its list of the 50 Greatest American Screen Legends, Bogart was at the top of the list. His persona as a tough guy who manages to maintain his sense of virtue no matter how compromising the situation features in some of the most famous films ever made, including *Casablanca* (1942), *The Maltese Falcon* (1941), and *Key Largo* (1949).

Bogart's screen persona was not only desirable (everyone wanted to be like Bogart) but also highly approachable, in the sense that he played the everyman figure far more than Cary Grant or Laurence Olivier, for example. Bogart also had good timing, with some of his popularity due to the fact that he rose to fame in an era when the film industry was at its most potent. Bogart's prime coincided with the Golden Age of cinema; sound had been successfully integrated and the studio system ruled over the industry. Bogart was the biggest star at a time in which the medium itself held immense mass appeal, and he has been famous ever since.

People have long been familiar with Bogart's career and movies, but the differences between his persona and his real life are also interesting. Bogart's everyman screen persona belies the fact that he came from immense privilege, and his down-to-earth film roles are in many ways a rebellion against a family with which he was never close. There were traits that Bogart inherited from his parents, but his film career also offered Bogart to escape a family culture that was antithetical to his personality. Bogart's screen persona as a jaded but ultimately indestructible figure also obscures the fact that his life was filled with substantial tragedy, culminating in his own premature death at the age of 57. Separating Bogart's real life from his reel life is still a subject of great interest and debate.

Hollywood's Gangster Icons profiles the life, career, and legacy of the man deemed by the American Film Institute as the greatest male star. Along with pictures of important people, places, and events, you will learn about Humphrey Bogart like you never have before.

Cagney in *G-Men* (1935)

James Cagney (1899-1986)

"You don't psych yourself up for these things, you do them...I'm acting for the audience, not for myself, and I do it as directly as I can." – James Cagney

When the American Film Institute assembled its top 100 actors of all time at the close of the 20th century, one of the Top 10 was James Cagney, an actor whose acting and dancing talents spawned a stage and film career that spanned over 5 decades and once compelled Orson Welles to call him "maybe the greatest actor to ever appear in front of a camera." Indeed, his portrayal of "The Man Who Owns Broadway", George M. Cohan, earned him an Academy Award in the musical *Yankee Doodle Dandy*, and as famed director Milos Forman once put it, "I think he's some kind of genius. His instinct, it's just unbelievable. I could just stay at home. One of the qualities of a brilliant actor is that things look better on the screen than the set. Jimmy has that quality."

Ultimately, it was portraying tough guys and gangsters in the 1930s that turned Cagney into a massive Hollywood star, and they were the kind of roles he was literally born to play after growing up rough in Manhattan at the turn of the 20th century. In movies like *The Public Enemy* (which included the infamous "grapefruit scene") and *White Heat*, Cagney convincingly and grippingly played criminals that brought Warner to the forefront of Hollywood and the gangster genre. Cagney also helped pave the way for younger actors in the genre, like Humphrey Bogart, and he was so good that he found himself in danger of being typecast.

While Cagney is no longer remembered as fondly or as well as Bogart, he was also crucial in helping establish the system in which actors worked as independent workers free from the constraints of studios. Refusing to be pushed around, Cagney was constantly involved in contract squabbles with Warner, and he often came out on top, bucking the conventional system that saw studios treat their stars as indentured servants who had to make several films a year.

Hollywood's Gangster Icons examines the life and career of one of Hollywood's most iconic actors. Along with pictures of important people, places, and events, you will learn about Cagney like never before.

Edward G. Robinson (1893-1973)

"I know I'm not much on face value, but when it comes to stage value, I'll deliver for you." – Edward G. Robinson

For most enthusiasts of film history, Edward G. Robinson's name is virtually synonymous with the Depression-era gangster films of the 1930s. After all, Robinson starred in *Little Caesar* (1931), which was one of the first major gangster films and is perhaps the most representative example of the genre. *Little Caesar* remains his most iconic gangster role, but he acted in several other notable gangster films over the course of the decade, including *The Little Giant* (1933) and *A Slight Case of Murder* (1938). Even during the 1940s, after the gangster genre had ceded much of its standing to the postwar film noir genre, Robinson retained his ties to gangster films, memorably playing gangster Johnny Rocco in *Key Largo* (1948). With his short, round physique and irascible screen persona, Robinson became a kind of cinematic brother to James Cagney, and the two remain the most famous of the Hollywood gangster stars.

As much as Robinson's fame remains attached to the rise of the gangster films of the 1930s, it also is important to recognize that he was successful in progressing into the postwar noir films—

a genre that bears important similarities with the gangster genre but reworks it in significant ways. Indeed, Robinson starred in what may have been the most famous gangster picture – he played a memorable role in *Double Indemnity* (1944), which may well be the most famous noir movie ever made. Edward established his status as a worthy noir actor by starring in a duo of underrated Fritz Lang films—*The Woman in the Window* (1944) and *Scarlet Street* (1945)—as well as the Orson Welles movie *The Stranger* (1946). As his memorable noir performances demonstrate, Edward G. Robinson was more than just a famous gangster villain. He represents someone who was able to successfully navigate the changes in Hollywood cinema from the 1930s through the following decade.

Interestingly, even as Robinson became a star on the screen, events off screen also made him abdicate his lofty standing. A first-generation immigrant who moved to the United States from Romania while still a child, Robinson's rise in the entertainment industry—first on stage and then in Hollywood—embodied the Horatio Alger myth of a self-made man. Lacking the conventional attractiveness that characterized most male actors (particularly leading men), it was through his sheer skill and virtuosity that Robinson was able to fashion a successful career. However, if Robinson benefited early in his career from the opportunities presented by Hollywood, it was also at the hands of the industry that his career was compromised during the early 1950s through the efforts of the House Un-American Activities Committee (HUAC). Although he was not a member of the Hollywood Ten, Robinson was a suspected Communist, and his name was tarnished within the acting community and in the eyes of the American public. He would continue to act through the end of his life, but his days as a major figure in Hollywood were brought to an abrupt end.

Hollywood's Gangster Icons analyzes Robinson's career in the 1930s and 1940s, as well as his real life roles as Hollywood star and victim.. Along with pictures and a bibliography, you will learn about Edward G. Robinson like never before.

Hollywood's Gangster Icons: The Lives and Careers of Humphrey Bogart, James Cagney, and Edward G. Robinson

Humphrey Bogart

Chapter 1: Early Years

One of the most shocking aspects of Humphrey Bogart's life story is the discrepancy between his roles on screen and his family background. Humphrey was the eldest child of Belmont DeForest Bogart and Maud Humphrey, and he would later have two younger sisters, Frances and Catherine. Humphrey's father was a Presbyterian with Dutch and English ancestry whose last name was Dutch for "keeper of an orchard", but Belmont worked as a cardiopulmonary surgeon and came from a privileged family background. He had also descended from a family with historical ties to the landscape, as his family had arrived in Brooklyn from Holland in the 17th century. Humphrey's grandfather, Adam Watkins Bogart, ran an inn in the Finger Lakes region in upstate New York, and in 1853 the family had relocated to upstate New York from Brooklyn. Adam descended from a lineage of farmers, but Humphrey's paternal grandmother had come from a wealthy background herself.

Belmont was born in 1866, just one year following the death of his brother. His mother would die just two years after his birth and left all of her wealth to her son. But interestingly, in her will she asked that Belmont be removed from her husband's possession and placed in the custody of one of her sisters. Adam eventually sued her estate and won, regaining custody over his son. With his inheritance, Belmont was sure to enjoy a comfortable upbringing, and his father Adam made a fortune from creating a method for lithographing plates, but the unusual episode surrounding the will and Belmont's custody demonstrated the coldness of his parents' marriage. That lack of affection would also be especially relevant in Humphrey Bogart's life.

It is believed that Humphrey was born on Christmas Day in 1899, but the story has faced much dissension over the years because it seemed too good to be true. For a long time, many people thought Humphrey's Christmas Day birthday was a myth fabricated by Warner Brothers to add to his allure. The alternative theory was that he was born in late January 1900, but documents from the period suggest he was definitely born in December 1899. While movie studios often changed their stars' names and other pertinent information, based on his movie roles it would seem as though Bogart lacked the kind of sweet nature that would drive the studio to fabricate that story out of thin air.

Bogart's unusual first name was borrowed from his mother's maiden name. Maud Humphrey was of English origin and Episcopalian faith. She was also considered an extraordinarily beautiful woman, with vivid red hair. Her father was a wealthy shoe manufacturer, and she grew up even more privileged than her husband. Given the era Maud grew up in, she was a very strong and career-oriented woman, and she was also an avowed suffragette who never submitted to the male-dominated norms of the time period.

Maud's parents had sent her to art school, where she became an accomplished illustrator. After graduating from school and marrying Belmont, she worked as a commercial illustrator, where she earned a robust salary of $50,000 per year, more than double her husband's not-insignificant salary. Naturally, Maud drew pictures of her baby boy, one of which was featured in an ad campaign for Mellins Baby Food. Humphrey would later wryly note, "There was a period in American history when you couldn't pick up a goddamned magazine without seeing my kisser in it."

Maud and Humphrey

Humphrey as a boy

Since they were each so independently driven, Bogart's parents were never close or affectionate, and they sparred continuously, unleashing sarcastic quips on each other that made them seem more like rivals than loving parents. Humphrey clearly inherited his own caustic wit from his parents, but as a young child he suffered from lack of attention. As Humphrey put it, "I was brought up very unsentimentally but very straightforwardly. A kiss, in our family, was an event. Our mother and father didn't glug over my two sisters and me."

In fact, with his parents constantly working, Humphrey was largely raised by a collection of housekeepers and caretakers. His parents eschewed all manner of physical or verbal affection, keeping a cold distance from him that would never grow more intimate, even after their son rose to fame. Humphrey explained, "If, when I was grown up, I sent my mother one of those Mother's Day telegrams or said it with flowers, she would have returned the wire and flowers to me, collect."

Despite their professional strength and standing in the New York society realm, Humphrey's parents were physically fragile figures. Maud suffered from debilitating headaches, while Belmont was addicted to morphine, a condition that would later play a strong role in his demise. When both were at home, they continuously fought with one another, no doubt in part due to the fact that they often didn't feel well.

Of course, Humphrey's privileged upbringing had enormous advantages that were counterbalanced by significant disadvantages. He came from a highly respected family that lived in a posh Upper West Side apartment in Manhattan and was listed in *Dua's New York Blue Book*. The block Humphrey grew up on has since been ceremonially renamed Humphrey Bogart Place. Naturally there were aspects of his family's wealth that Humphrey enjoyed. Chief among these was the family's summer stays at their 55-acre estate in Canandaigua in upstate New York. The family held a prominent role in the summer community, and their arrival and departure was fodder for the newspaper. While summering, he was introduced to major society figures, including future president Franklin Delano Roosevelt.

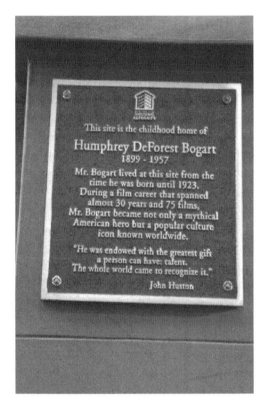

Plaque at Bogart's childhood home on W. 103rd St.

In 1913, when Bogart was still 13 years old, his family switched summer homes, relocating to Fire Island in order to be closer to Maud's job in New York City. In 1910, she had assumed the prestigious role of artistic director for the fashion magazine *The Delineator*. At Fire Island, Bogart became friends with the other residents, staged theatrical productions with them, and met his first girlfriend there. One of his closest friends was William Brady Jr., who would play an instrumental role later in his life. Brady was the closest friend Bogart would have during his youth, and the two were given free tickets to Broadway shows by Brady's father, entertainment mogul William Brady Sr. It has even been suggested that the friendship between Bogart and Brady was at times homoerotic. Most importantly, summering on the water engendered a deep love for boating, and Humphrey became particularly adept at sailing, a passion that would remain with him for the rest of his life.

Humphrey was quite happy during the summer, but he lived in relative misery during the other parts of the year. The thing that stood out most about young Humphrey was that his mother insisted on dressing him in precious clothes that had long become antiquated by the time he was born. Humphrey also grew to resent his name, which quickly became a source of ridicule among his classmates. Making matters worse, another source of self-consciousness stemmed from the fact that as a young child, Maud had illustrated her son in the nude from behind, a drawing that became famous and was disseminated throughout the country. Although Maud refrained from giving her son loving attention and their relationship was quite distant, it is also apparent that Humphrey was monitored too closely by his mother, who did not give him the agency to dress and present himself in a manner that would endear him to his classmates. His famous lisp, which would later become one of his trademarks as an actor, caused ridicule from his classmates, as did his curly hair. As a result, Humphrey was perpetually viewed as a pretty boy and an outsider; one classmate said of him, "Bogart never came out for anything. He wasn't a very good student... He added up to nothing in our class."

Given that his time at school was another source of discomfort, it is no surprise that Humphrey shunned his studies even at an early age. At first, he attended the Delancey School, where he matriculated until the 5th grade. Bogart then enrolled in Trinity School, an elite all-boys school that had already been in existence for 200 years by the time Humphrey went there in 1909. While attending Trinity School, Bogart was required to don a blue suit, a style of dress he would retain for the rest of his life. He attended Trinity for a full 8 years, during which time he performed poorly and was forced to repeat the 11th grade after having suffered from scarlet fever. After returning from school, Humphrey would pose for his mother, who would draw him in her studio. This curious dynamic, in which Humphrey was fodder for her illustrations, has led plenty of people to suggest that Humphrey's first experience as an actor was in his own home.

Despite attending prestigious schools, Humphrey always believed that school was not the appropriate environment for him. Even so, his parents had high aspirations that he would follow in his father's footsteps and become a doctor, so there was immense pressure on Bogart to perform well in school. The family also regularly entertained literary luminaries like Theodore Dreiser and H.L. Mencken, and Humphrey was an articulate and avid reader, so his lack of academic success greatly frustrated his parents. In a sense, his perpetual lack of achievement in school was a form of rebellion against his parents and his early years more than an expression of poor intelligence.

By the time Bogart neared the end of his high school studies, it was clear that he would need assistance in order to gain admittance to a prestigious college. Therefore, Belmont used his connections to have Humphrey admitted at Philips Andover Academy in Massachusetts, where Humphrey was to matriculate for his final year of high school and eventually attend medical school at Yale University. However, Belmont's best-laid plans were not realized, and the year at Andover was a tumultuous whirlwind of interactions between Humphrey, Belmont, and the school's headmaster. Ultimately, Humphrey was expelled just one month before graduating and was offered no option to repeat the year.

School was clearly a source of unhappiness for Humphrey, so his expulsion from Andover would come to be a welcome occurrence for him, especially because it effectively terminated his parents' delusional view that their son would grow up to be a surgeon. After failing to complete even the one year at Andover, they were finally forced to acknowledge that school was not the proper venue for their son. In this regard, the year at Andover was a sort of success for Humphrey.

Chapter 2: On His Own

"At 18, war was great stuff. Paris! French girls! Hot damn!...The war was a big joke. Death? What does death mean to a 17 year old?" – Humphrey Bogart

After his year ended prematurely at Andover, Maud secured her son a job working for a naval architect. Uninterested in this line of work, or in having his parents decide his profession, Humphrey lasted a very short time there; in fact, some people assert that he never actually worked there at all. In an act of youthful exuberance and rebellion against his parents, Bogart instead decided to enlist in the Navy.

Bogart in the Navy

For someone who had vehemently resisted authority all throughout his life, it may initially come as a surprise that he would choose to enlist in the Navy, which meant he would have to obey authority. However, Bogart knew that he loved ships, and he also wanted to travel overseas and explore the world. In the early summer of 1918, he enlisted and was stationed at the Naval Reserve Training Station in Pelham Bay, off the coast of New York.

While at Pelham Bay, Bogart was unable to progress through the ranks and eventually applied for a transfer to the Naval Aviation branch, but he was denied admission. In reality, Bogart's glamorous fantasies about World War I were ill-founded. By the time he enlisted, the Armistice had already been signed, and he eventually joined the USS *Leviathan*, where he spent 8 months transporting troops back and forth from overseas. It was the least glamorous naval job imaginable, but Bogart finally acquired a sense of discipline and commitment, and there is every indication that his experience there was vastly preferable to his time at Andover and Trinity.

Humphrey may also have received the scarred lip that became his trademark while serving on the *Leviathan*. The most common tale claims that a prisoner of war hit Bogart in the face with his handcuffs while being transferred to Kittery, Maine, but that story has not been verified and there are many conflicting reports, including one that asserts his lip was hit by a piece of shrapnel. Actor David Niven claimed Bogart told him his lip was scarred as a child and the Navy story was made up by movie studios to add to Bogart's persona. Either way, the scarred lip also contributed to Bogart's lisp.

In 1919, Bogart was transferred to the USS *Santa Olivia*, but he failed to show up for the boat's departure for Europe, a serious naval offense that earned him the label of Deserter. Bogart admitted to the transgression, but turning himself in to the authorities was not enough to overturn his punishment. He was forced to draw on more desperate measures. Relying on his family's connections with Franklin D. Roosevelt, who was then Assistant Secretary of the Navy, Humphrey contacted the future president. Taking pity on his family acquaintance, Roosevelt exercised his authority and had Bogart's punishment changed to Absent without Leave. For his actions, he was stationed in solitary confinement for three days, the standard punishment for going AWOL, but the lighter punishment allowed Bogart to be honorably discharged. Bogart was even given a medal for his efforts in the service.

After returning from the Navy, Bogart was still just 19 years old, and he still did not possess even a high school education. Making matters worse, his family's economic situation was in shambles. His father's addiction to morphine had become more severe, and he had begun to lose his mental acuity. In a bizarre move, his father had invested in a foolish business opportunity involving timber, losing the family fortune and falling massively into debt. As a last resort, Belmont was relegated to serving as a ship doctor. Nevertheless, Belmont's travails and the collapse of the family's wealth didn't particularly devastate Humphrey; outside of the family's summer home, he had always resented their upper class trimmings. Bogart had never cared for the pretentious ways the family's wealth had provided for the family, even though he had used money and connections to pull strings a few times himself.

Even if his father was unable to subsidize him, Belmont did use his influence to secure his son a job as a bond salesman. After this occupation proved unsuccessful, Humphrey called upon William Brady Sr., the father of his childhood friend. By this point, Brady had become immensely powerful and was looking to spread his empire from the theater to the motion picture industry. He had founded the motion picture company World Films, where he made a fortune capitalizing on the popularity of the seventh art. Brady offered Bogart a position in his office, where he was paid $35 per week, $5 more than he had made as a bond salesman.

Bogart committed himself to the job with greater diligence than any prior period in his life, and he was immediately successful. After just one month in the office, Humphrey was promoted to the role of production manager, a shift that earned him a salary increase to $50 per week. While with World Films, Bogart conducted a number of tasks, including arranging for props and paying the actors. Eventually, he even served as producer and director, and did screenwriting as well.

Although he enjoyed his time at World Films, Bogart was always more interested in acting. As the 1920s progressed, Bogart began appearing in theatrical productions in New York City. It was clear to everyone, including his reluctant parents, that Bogart was a natural actor; in one of his first performances, Belmont noted of his son, "The boy's good, isn't he?" Still, Bogart was unpolished enough at first that it was also apparent he had plenty of work to do yet.

Bogart was drawn to city life, and the acting lifestyle suited him perfectly. He had begun drinking while in high school, but acting allowed him to drink heavily without losing his job. Bogart spent ample time in speakeasies and became increasingly attached to drinking bourbon and smoking cigarettes. He would later quip, "The whole world is three drinks behind. If everyone in the world would take three drinks, we would have no trouble. If Stalin, Truman and everybody else in the world had three drinks right now, we'd all loosen up and we wouldn't need the United Nations."

Bogart had watched his parents drink heavily, but his own heavy drinking was likely due more to his youth and rebellious personality. The fact that Prohibition was just going into effect only encouraged Bogart to drink more. Bogart and William Brady Jr. became notorious for spending most of their nights at speakeasies in New York, and Bogart was able to partially fund his drinking by challenging bar patrons to chess games for $1 each. When he was strapped for money, the young man frequently managed to talk his way into having the owners put his drinks on a long-running tab. Bogart spent so much time at bars that he constantly fell asleep in them, and some contemporaries claimed his scarred lip came from a barroom brawl.

To Bogart's credit, the long nights and heavy drinking didn't stop him from securing relatively consistent acting opportunities. But Humphrey was repeatedly cast in roles that he found disagreeable, performing in what he would later refer to as "White Pants Willie" roles. Ironically, these stage roles represented the antithesis of the rugged characters he would later portray on film, and it seems his family background made it difficult for him to shed the soft, non-masculine roles he kept being assigned on stage.

Bogart may have thought his career was still less than satisfactory, but his personal life underwent significant developments during the 1920s. While acting in a performance of *Drifting* at the Playhouse Theatre in 1922, he met actress Helen Menken, who he would later marry on May 20, 1926 at the Gramercy Park Hotel in New York City.

Helen Menken

Their marriage was doomed from the start and would last roughly 18 months. Menken was 10 years older than him, and her domineering personality clashed with young Bogart's independent streak. The time he spent at bars made adultery much easier, and he admitted, "I had had enough women by the time I was 27 to know what I was looking for in a wife the next time I married."

Despite what he said, the second marriage didn't go much better. Following his divorce, Bogart met Mary Philips, another actress. Philips was closer in age to Bogart and could drink nearly as much as him, something that was actually considered an asset by her husband, but she was similar in many respects to Menken too, particularly her quick temper. Bogart and Philips had known each other since before he had married Menken, after they performed together in a production of *Nerves* at the Comedy Theatre in 1924. He and Mary would remain married for nearly a decade, but their marriage was hardly a happy one. Bogart was perpetually unfaithful and slept with many women, a dynamic that would continue until he met Lauren Bacall nearly two decades later. More noteworthy, the marriage between two strong-willed individuals reproduced the unhappy marital dynamic that had compromised his parents' own marriage. For whatever reason, Bogart's early marriages were filled with the same friction that had subsumed Belmont and Maud, and he was unable to adhere to the strict routines of domestic life.

Mary Philips

Bogart's career was less than ideal during the 1920s, but it was still possible for a stage actor to earn a decent living during most of the decade. However, this would change with the stock market crash and the onset of the Great Depression. Suddenly, the upper-middle class demographic that the industry had relied upon was gone, and stage actors were forced to search for new opportunities. Fortunately, the collapse of the theater coincided with the emergence of the Motion Picture industry, which by this time was in the process of converting to synchronized sound.

There were many reasons for the emergence of film and its ability to flourish even during the Great Depression. First, film had always marketed itself as a more democratic medium than theater; although film borrowed from theater, it also had roots in more traditionally working class forms of entertainment like the circus and the vaudeville stage. From an economic standpoint, movies were cheaper to attend, and even those who were strapped for money were able to save up and see at least one movie a week. Moreover, the inherent dreamlike quality of film, with spectators sitting in a dark movie house, afforded viewers a sense of escape that was not possible in the theater.

At first, Bogart was unsuccessful in finding consistent employment in the movies. He was able to secure minor roles in two Vitaphone shorts, *The Dancing Town* (1928) (which also starred Mary Philips) and *Broadway's Like That* (1930). In the first film, a 20-minute two-reel production, Bogart plays himself. Meanwhile, *Broadway's Like That* involves a girl finding out on the night before her marriage that her husband (played by Bogart) is already married. Despite these two roles, lasting employment evaded him, and Bogart grew increasingly depressed. He was trapped in an unhappy marriage and lacked consistent acting opportunities.

Finally, Bogart was hired by the Fox Film Cooperative in 1930, where he earned a lucrative salary of $750 per week, a substantial amount of money during the Great Depression. He began to appear in films on a continuous basis, but he also acted in the theater as well. He appeared in John Ford's early film *Up the River* (1930), during which he met then-unknown actor Spencer Tracy, who would later become one of his closest friends. The next year, he acted in *The Bad Sister*, playing a minor role in the film, which starred Bette Davis.

Spencer Tracy

However, after his contract with Fox expired, Bogart again found himself without work and he spiraled into a deep depression. For the next four years, he would alternate between theater and cinema, but he suffered from extended bouts of unemployment the entire time. Bogart continued to drink heavily, and conditions were made even worse when his parents separated and his father died. Belmont's death left Bogart with substantial debt, placing him in a position of outright economic desperation. One friend later recalled seeing Bogart drinking himself into a stupor at a low-scale bar in the city and saying to her friend, "Poor Humphrey, he's finally licked."

Chapter 3: Breakthrough

By 1934, Bogart's life had reached its nadir. He had incurred his father's debt, was involved in a loveless marriage, and could not find consistent employment. In light of these circumstances, it is worth asking exactly how Bogart was able to catapult himself to fame.

One answer is that the poverty he experienced throughout the latter part of the decade effectively shed his label as a spoiled youth. Bogart had always shunned the title, but after actually experiencing poverty, he was finally able to capture the essence of a hardened everyman. Additionally, the advent of sound cinema played an integral role in transforming Bogart's identity. If vestiges of the spoiled, bourgeois young adult remained in his appearance, they were swiftly counteracted by his throaty voice, which grew increasingly coarser through his persistent smoking habits. Bogart's appearance eventually became iconic, but his voice played at least an equal role in catapulting him to fame.

It was not until 1934 that Bogart earned his breakthrough role, and it was on the stage. While Bogart acted in the Broadway play *Invitation to Murder* at the Theatre Marque in 1934, stage producer Arthur Hopkins learned of his role. Bogart auditioned for a role in Hopkins' *The Petrified Forest* completely hungover and looking like he had just spent all night at a bar, which he had. But the scruffy look was exactly what Hopkins was looking for, so he decided to cast Bogart to play an escaped convict in the theatrical production of *The Petrified Forest*. Hopkins mentioned just how different Bogart looked compared to the previous roles he had performed, "When I saw the actor I was somewhat taken aback, for he was the one I never much admired. He was an antiquated juvenile who spent most of his stage life in white pants swinging a tennis racquet. He seemed as far from a cold-blooded killer as one could get, but the voice (dry and tired) persisted, and the voice was Mantee's."

The play enjoyed a long run, with 197 performances at the Broadhurst Theatre in New York City, and Bogart received critical acclaim for his realistic portrayal of a madman. His role was substantially different from the film roles that would make him famous. After all, he played a man with no moral compass and was celebrated for his ability to shock audiences, leaving viewers terrified by him rather than identifying with him. Bogart was well aware that it was his breakthrough role, claiming that the role "marked my deliverance from the ranks of the sleek, sybaritic, stiff-shirted, swallow-tailed 'smoothies' to which I seemed condemned to life."

The show's enduring run also led to *The Petrified Forest* receiving a film adaptation from Warner Brothers, but casting for the film adaptation was not as simple as transferring the actors from the stage to the screen because there were studio politics at work. Warner Brothers felt obligated to feature their premium talent; because of the play's success, the studio envisioned the film as a major box office hit and intended to deploy their most famous actors. During this period, every studio had a different niche that was aligned with a particular genre. MGM was renowned for its musicals, but Warner Brothers was associated with gangster and crime films. The studio's most notable actors were Edward G. Robinson, George Raft, James Cagney, and Paul Muni, and all of them were associated with the gangster genre. For the film version of *The Petrified Forest*, the studio had originally wanted Edward G. Robinson to play Bogart's role. Given their substantial differences in appearance and star image, it is easy to retroactively deride the studio for intending to cast Robinson, but at this time there were few actors in Hollywood with more renown, and audiences expected to watch a Warner Brothers film with at least one major gangster actor in it.

Nevertheless, Bogart was dejected after learning that he was not going to be included in the film. In an act of desperation, he contacted Leslie Howard, with whom he had starred in the play and who was also set to star in the film, and informed him of the news. Howard had been fond of Bogart in the play and contacted Jack Warner, after which Bogart was given the role.

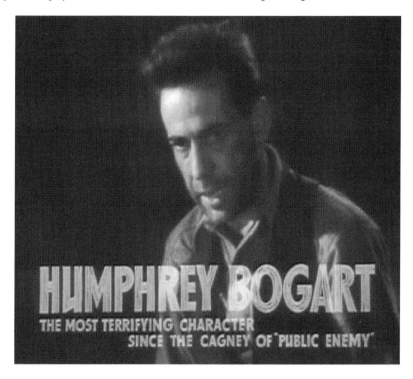

Publicity still shot of Bogart in *The Petrified Forest*

The film version of *The Petrified Forest* (1936) proved to be an even greater career milestone for Bogart than the play had been, not because the film garnered any acclaim but because it solidified Bogart's place with the studio. He would remain with Warner Brothers for roughly the next 15 years. Beginning with a salary of $550 per week, he would keep rising through the studio's ranks until he became the highest-paid actor in Hollywood in 1946. Bogart terrified audiences in his role as Duke Mantee, the escaped convict who takes customers at a roadside diner hostage. The film is hardly remembered today, but it was a relatively significant production that starred Bette Davis in addition to the aforementioned Bogart and Leslie Howard.

Leslie Howard and Bette Davis

One of the more interesting developments that took place during the production of *The Petrified Forest* is that Jack Warner attempted to get Bogart to adopt a stage name, but he refused. Considering his ambivalence toward the name "Humphrey," it is surprising that Bogart did not adopt a new moniker, and there is no ready explanation as to why he kept the name. After all, the reasons why the studio suggested a name change were the same reasons why Bogart had always despised his first name: it was not masculine enough. It is possible that Bogart kept his name as an act of deference toward his mother, but he never spoke fondly of her and it doesn't seem likely that he would have felt any obligation toward her. Moreover, at this point in his career, Bogart held absolutely no leverage within the film industry, particularly considering the fact that he was only in the film because the leading star had forced the studio's hand. Perhaps the best explanation is that by 1936, Bogart was no longer young and it would have been too drastic a change for someone in the middle of his life.

In a sense, the rest of the decade would prove to be Bogart's most prolific period. He had not yet reached the popularity that he would later enjoy, but there was no busier period of his career. Over the course of his career, Bogart would act in over 80 films, and the vast majority of them came during the latter half of the 1930s. As a result, it is important to remember how substantially different the film industry was during the 1930s from how it is today. After an actor signed a contract with the studio, they effectively operated as indentured servants, appearing in an unlimited number of films at the discretion of the studio, who could drop them at any point in time. For this reason, from 1936-1940, Bogart averaged a film every two months, and it was not uncommon for him to appear in multiple films at once.

Bogart was typecast as a gangster villain, which ensured that he had constant work but also prevented him from becoming a star. He was a subordinate to actors like Robinson, Cagney, and Raft, who had been involved in the gangster genre for a longer period of time. Therefore, while the 1930s were the busiest phase of his career, being relegated to a narrow character type meant that he was unable to truly display his acting talents. Bogart claimed, "I can't get in a mild discussion without turning it into an argument. There must be something in my tone of voice, or this arrogant face—something that antagonizes everybody. Nobody likes me on sight. I suppose that's why I'm cast as the heavy."

Many of the films Bogart acted in from 1936-1940 are largely forgotten, but by the end of the decade he had appeared in some of the most acclaimed films in the genre. In 1938, he appeared in *Angels with Dirty Faces* alongside James Cagney, and in 1939 he held substantial roles in *The Roaring Twenties* (also with Cagney) and *Dark Victory* (with Bette Davis). In these films, there is no mistaking that Bogart was not the leading star, but he became a more recognizable face, albeit one who was forced to assimilate within the character norms of the gangster genre.

Bogart and Cagney in *The Roaring Twenties*

During the latter half of the 1930s, major changes occurred within Bogart's personal life as well. In 1937, he divorced Mary Philips, ending their perpetually tumultuous relationship. The following year, he married Mayo Methot, another stage actress whose heavy drinking was coupled with a fiery temper. Methot was yet another woman with a personality like his mother's, but Bogart's third wife had an even more erratic temper. While at times she could be quite charming, she was also prone to immense bouts of anger and was often abusive to Bogart. Over the course of their marriage, she committed a number of incidents that in most any other marriage would have been grounds for divorce, including stabbing Bogart, threatening to kill him, and setting their house on fire. Bogart could be just as abusive, and one friend quipped, "The Bogart-Methot marriage was the sequel to the Civil War". Even the press was well aware of the marital troubles, dubbing them "the battling Bogarts", and their household also became known as Sluggy Hollow. It was one of the few places Bogart and Methot could go after awhile, because places started to ban them to avoid public fighting.

Mayo Methot would drink herself to death by the age of 47.

It is difficult to determine why Bogart was drawn to such women, but some of it may have stemmed from his inherent dislike for the bourgeois nuclear family. With nontraditional wives, Bogart prevented his life from falling into the staid rhythms of the upper crust lifestyle he had always shunned. For his part, Bogart often played it off, claiming that he liked having a jealous wife and asserting, "I wouldn't give you two cents for a dame without a temper." Besides, Bogart also had a reputation for being prickly, to the extent that plenty of people in Hollywood went out of their way to avoid him, even as the media lapped up his candid statements. He explained, "All over Hollywood, they are continually advising me, 'Oh, you mustn't say that. That will get you in a lot of trouble,' when I remark that some picture or writer or director or producer is no good. I don't get it. If he isn't any good, why can't you say so? If more people would mention it, pretty soon it might start having some effect."

Chapter 4: Hollywood Stardom

"An actor needs something to stabilize his personality, something to nail down what he really is, not what he is currently pretending to be." – Humphrey Bogart

It would not be until 1940 that Bogart caught his big break. That year, he was given a prominent starring role in *They Drive by Night* (1940). Directed by Raoul Walsh, the film cast Bogart and George Raft as brothers who operate their own truck-driving business. The film marked a dramatic shift away from gangster films and toward a more socially realistic style that portrayed Bogart with greater pathos than his earlier roles. One scene in particular, in which he falls asleep behind the wheel while transporting an overloaded truck filled with cargo, is especially suspenseful and conveys Bogart and Raft as everymen forced to go to extremes to make ends meet. Although the film's chief romantic grouping is between George Raft and Ida Lupino, Bogart serves as a sympathetic co-star rather than simply acting as a foil for the leading actor, and the role is substantially more significant than his earlier ones. With *They Drive By Night*, audiences finally became exposed to a more sensitive side to the actor, a dimension that would obviously emerge even further as the decade progressed.

Bogart's next film was even more significant. After starring with him in *They Drive By Night*, Ida Lupino cast him in *High Sierra* (1941), another film that deployed elements of the gangster genre while portraying its heroes in a sympathetic light. In the film, Bogart plays a man who has just been released from prison (a motif that recalls his role in *The Petrified Forest*) and is forced into reentering the mob since they engineered his release. He is then asked to take part in a major heist and acquiesces out of desperation. The heist fails, and Bogart falls in love with Ida Lupino's character, ultimately sacrificing himself to save her at the film's conclusion. The tragic hero is a trope of the gangster film, and in this regard Bogart's death would appear to make the film a classic example of the genre. However, in most gangster films the death of the criminal signals the victory of justice, whereas in *High Sierra*, Bogart's death elicits sympathy from the viewer. Consequently, *High Sierra* had a nuanced portrayal of morality, in which the viewer is forced to think outside traditional notions of good vs. evil and consider the obstacles facing a convict who is relegated to serving in the mob even after he has outgrown it and is ready to reform.

High Sierra was not a box office sensation, but it did show Hollywood that Bogart was capable of playing a leading role. Moreover, his experience acting in the film had placed Bogart in contact with John Huston, who had written the script for Lupino's film. Although he would later enjoy a famously prolific career, at the start of the 1940s Huston had not yet directed. Fortunately for him, he had the opportunity to direct *The Maltese Falcon*, a film based on a superlative pulp fiction novel by Dashiell Hammett and for which he wrote the script. Huston knew that he wanted Bogart for the starring role of Sam Spade, a world-weary detective who cannot trust anyone and is forced to solve a mystery in which nothing is as it appears.

Huston

With *The Maltese Falcon*, Bogart fully portrayed the screen persona for which he would become an icon. Although Bogart's Sam Spade is a member of law enforcement, he also defies conventional standards of behavior and morality, as evidenced by his famous quote, "I stick my neck out for nobody." In particular, his disregard for chivalry enables him to suspect that the leading female character (played by Mary Astor) is the individual responsible for the murders that take place. In his essay "The Hero", Manny Farber offers a perceptive analysis of Bogart's character and the complications associated with the star persona:

> "The hero played by Mr. Bogart, which grew out of the gangster film and Dashiell Hammett detective novels, looks as though he had been knocked around daily and had spent his week-ends drinking himself unconscious in the back rooms of saloons. His favorite grimace is a hateful pulling back of the lips from his clenched teeth, and when his lips are together he seems to be holding back a mouthful of blood. The people he acts badly toward and spends his movie life exposing as fools are mainly underworld characters, like gangsters, cabaret owners and dance-hall girls (and the mayor whom he puts into office every year). Everything he does carries conflicting quantities of hatred and love, as though he felt you had just stepped on his face but hadn't meant it....He is the soured half of the American dream, which believes that if you are good, honest and persevering you will win the kewpie doll".

Bogart's role renewed the focus on psychological realism that was initiated in *They Drive By Night* and *High Sierra*. While the traditional law enforcement character works to maintain the façade of the American Dream, there is the sense that Bogart's character has undergone too much suffering to subscribe to such an idea. It is as though he sees the world as it is rather than how it should be. Bogart was especially proud of the film, calling it "practically a masterpiece" and adding, "I don't have many things I'm proud of...but that's one."

Trailer image from *The Maltese Falcon*

After the success of *The Maltese Falcon*, Bogart's stock had soared, and he was now nearly on top of Hollywood. Another helpful factor for him was that the United States was fighting World War II, and many of the leading actors were fighting overseas. While actors such as Kirk Douglas, Douglas Fairbanks, and Henry Fonda were gone abroad, Bogart was too old to join in the war effort, and he took full advantage of his opportunity. At the same time, Bogart provided a challenge for the Warner Brothers studio because he offered more versatility. Stars like Edward G. Robinson, James Cagney, and George Raft were all major box office attractions, but the studio basically reprised the well-worn formula of casting them as psychotic villains. Meanwhile, with Bogart the studio had a more valuable commodity, but also one who appeared too smart to believably cast as the flawed villain.

Bogart's next film, *Casablanca* (1942), would be one of the more ambitious films for Warner Brothers, as well as a major financial commitment. Hailed as an all-time classic, *Casablanca* was recognized as the number two Hollywood film of the 20th century by the American Film Institute when they comprised their list at the century's conclusion. There are many reasons for the film's continued acclaim, and chief among these was that the film perceptively captured the nation's ambivalence about going to war while at the same time recognizing that war was unavoidable.

Trailer screenshot of Bogart and Ingrid Bergman in _Casablanca_

As mentioned earlier, Warner Brothers was not only recognized for its gangster films but also for its social realist slant, and on the surface _Casablanca_ would appear to clash with this framework. There is no on-location shooting, and the interiors are easily discernible as studio sets. The film does not portray the gritty scenes of working-class life that characterized _They Drive By Night_ or _High Sierra_ either. Bogart played the role of Rick Blaine, an American expatriate operating a nightclub in Casablanca. After coming into possession of two tickets that grant permission to leave the country, he initially intends to take his ex-lover with him (Ilsa, played by Ingrid Bergman), but instead he eventually decides to give the tickets to Ilsa and her husband Victor (played by Paul Henreid), who the police want to arrest on specious charges. By refusing to leave the country with his beloved Ilsa, the film forgoes the classical narrative trope of the protagonist and heroine uniting at the film's conclusion. Instead, Bogart's character ends the film in much the same way as in _Maltese Falcon_: alone and world-weary.

The plot borrows heavily from other genres. First, the reconciliation between Rick and Ilsa superficially resembles the comedy-of-remarriage films that involved a romantic couple reuniting. Meanwhile, the cat-and-mouse game between the virtuous Laszlo and the villainous

Vichy Captain Louis Renault recalls the Warner Brothers gangster films of the preceding decade. As Manny Farber writes, "Before allied troops made it more famous, Casablanca served as a jumping-off spot to America for many of Europe's refugees—therefore a timely place to carry on Warner's favorite cops and robbers." Still, while it borrows from many different genres, the film derives its power through its ability to avoid the good vs. evil dichotomy that characterizes most gangster films. The zaniness of gangster films and screwball comedies is eschewed, and the film pours on as much emotion as possible.

One of the confounding (and appealing) aspects of *Casablanca* is that it achieves a level of psychological realism that few films have captured, yet it does so while adhering to an immense number of clichés. According to Umberto Eco, it is precisely through invoking an endless supply of clichés that *Casablanca* acquires its power: "But precisely because all the archetypes are here, precisely because *Casablanca* cites countless other films, and each actor plays a part played on other occasions, the resonance of intertextuality plays upon the spectator…When all the archetypes burst in shamelessly, we reach Homeric depths. Two clichés make us laugh. A hundred clichés move us."

The effect described by Eco has become even more pronounced in the years following the film's release. When the film is now screened, the audience is not only moved by the emotions specific to the film itself but also by the way in which archetypal scenes in the film (the famous "Play it Again, Sam" musical number, for example) have become embedded within American culture. For this reason, there is arguably no film that is more beloved in America, and the film completed the seemingly impossible task of outdoing *The Maltese Falcon* in terms of building Bogart's legend.

For *Casablanca*, Bogart was nominated for an Oscar, but he didn't win it. Bogart claimed he was fine with that, stating, "The best way to survive an Oscar is to never try to win another one. You've seen what happens to some Oscar winners. They spend the rest of their lives turning down scripts while searching for the great role to win another one. Hell, I hope I'm never even nominated again. It's meat-and-potato roles for me from now on."

Following *Casablanca*, Bogart finally broke his streak of successes, acting in four films of relatively minor acclaim. His next significant film was *To Have and Have Not* (1944), a film that was directed by Howard Hawks and co-starred his future wife, Lauren Bacall. Despite an age difference of nearly 25 years, Bogart and Bacall were instantly smitten with each other, and Hawks would claim "Bogie fell in love with the character she played, so she had to keep playing it the rest of her life."

Like many films of the 1930s and 1940s, the film was adapted from a book by a major literary giant, this one having been borrowed from Ernest Hemingway's novel of the same title. Even so, it would be misleading to simply declare Hawks' film as a straight adaptation of the famous book, because Hawks and Bogart applied their own trademarks to the film.

Bacall

Any analysis of Bogart's filmography must not only examine the actor himself but also the directors with whom he worked. To this end, it is important to note that the films Bogart acted in with John Huston are vastly different from those with Howard Hawks, reflecting the extent to which Bogart cannot be considered the sole author of his films. Where Huston's films are highly stylized and filmed with violence and virtuoso camera movements, Hawks' films are lighter in tone and deploy comedy to dramatic effect. In *To Have and Have Not*, Bogart and Bacall star as lovers who meet in Martinique after the collapse of France in 1940. Bogart plays a fishing-boat captain who transports members of the French resistance. While stationed in Martinique, he meets Marie "Slim" Browning (played by Bacall), with whom he falls in love.

Unlike *Casablanca*, Bogart ends the film with the love of his life, as it is implied that he and Bacall will spend the rest of their lives together. Another difference between *To Have and Have Not* and the earlier films is that Bogart displays a lighter side of his personality, referring to Bacall by the nickname "Slim" and engaging in courtship banter with her (most famously, when Bacall's character asks him if he knows how to whistle) that is reminiscent of the screwball comedy. In a sense, Hawks cast Bogart in the most desirable way imaginable; Bogart's role is playful enough to assume the role of a traditional leading man, but also rugged enough as a sailor and hard drinker that his masculinity is also on full display.

Moreover, despite the massive age difference between Bogart and Bacall, their witty repartee reflects a dynamic in which they treat each other as equals. In fact, Bacall is the character who more aggressively pursues the other, and her physique is more athletic and domineering as well. To this end, one of the most notable aspects of the film is the way in which Bogart is able to withhold his masculinity while also treating Bacall as his equal rather than his subordinate. Part of this was a conscious effort on Bogart's part to let Bacall steal scenes. The dynamic between the two of them was so appealing to audiences in *To Have and Have Not* that parts of their second film together, the classic *The Big Sleep*, were reshot to be racier.

The flirtatious dialogue of *To Have and Have Not* is not only characteristic of Hawks' style but also particularly apropos in light of the fact that Bogart and Bacall were also in love with one another off the film set. Despite still being married to Mayo Methot, Bogart and Bacall continued to date even after the film's production. Their courtship was not well-received by Howard Hawks, who was also in love with Bacall despite being married himself. Finally, Bogart and Methot divorced each other in 1945, something that was well overdue, and a few weeks later he married Bacall. Despite being just 45 years old, Bacall was his fourth wife. They moved into a gigantic white brick mansion in the posh neighborhood of Holmby Hills, California, and Bogart was happily married for the first time in his life.

Working with Hawks proved to be a wise move, and despite their conflict over their shared love interest, the Bogart, Hawks and Bacall triumvirate reunited once again for *The Big Sleep* (1946). Adapted from a novel by Raymond Chandler, the plot borrows elements from *The Maltese Falcon*. Bogart again played a detective (Philip Marlowe), and again he is non-committal. Nevertheless, there are significant differences between the two films, extending beyond the aesthetic tendencies of the two directors. While the plot of *The Maltese Falcon* is slow and protracted, *The Big Sleep* progresses at a breakneck speed that makes it difficult for viewers to keep track of the plot developments. Bogart's Philip Marlowe saves Bacall's character, Vivian, from being prosecuted for a murder she did not commit. At the same time, Vivian is the daughter of Bogart's client, which also serves as a reminder of the age discrepancy between Bogart and his much younger wife. The film concentrates on the romance between Bogart and Bacall to the extent that the murder plot becomes almost trivial, and in this vein, Pauline Kael notes that "sophisticated sex talk became the link for the movie, and the incidents and talk were so entertaining that audiences didn't care about the solution of the murder plot." In fact, one legend claimed that Raymond Chandler, the man who wrote the novel, couldn't answer who killed the limousine driver.

In the end, the film was another enormous success, and Humphrey Bogart was now the highest paid actor in Hollywood, commanding an unparalleled salary of $460,000. Furthermore, he commanded greater leverage in deciding on the films he appeared in. After appearing in three minor films, his next significant film was *Dark Passage* (1947), in which he plays the role of Vincent Parry, a man who has been convicted of murdering his wife and who subsequently escapes from the San Quentin Prison through a delivery truck. After meeting Irene Jansen (Bacall), Vincent falls in love with her, and they make plans to escape to South America together. It is easy to see why Bogart might have been attracted to take on the role, as there were similar plot elements to his earlier films. The escaped convict role recalls Bogart's character from *The Petrified Forest*, while the delivery truck calls to mind scenes from *They Drive By Night*. Ultimately, the film is above all a failed romance like *High Sierra*, as the romantic union between Bogart and Bacall will almost certainly be disrupted when Bogart is captured.

After the polished, fast-paced films with Hawks, it might seem surprising that Bogart would return to the grittiness of his earliest films, and in that regard *Dark Passage* is a somewhat perplexing film. At the same time, it is worth noting that Bogart had always preferred the dramatic style of John Huston over the zaniness of Howard Hawks. For this reason, it should come as no surprise that Huston would direct three of Humphrey's final films, all of which rank among the actor's most famous.

After *Dark Passage*, Bogart returned to Huston and appeared in *The Treasure of the Sierra Madre* (1948). It had been seven years since Bogart and Huston had joined forces in *The Maltese Falcon*, and now they were both giants in Hollywood. In light of this, it may come as a surprise that *The Treasure of the Sierra Madre* does not have the polish of the earlier film, but similar to *Dark Passage*, Bogart draws from the manic energy that had characterized his earliest films. In the film, he plays Dobbs, a man who goes to the Sierra Madre Mountains in Mexico with a friend to look for gold. Although he finds an ample amount of gold, he is consumed by paranoia and later killed. The film's methodical pace raises suspense in a manner similar to *The Maltese Falcon*, but the two films are quite different. While the earlier film featured Bogart in the smartest role, the later film casts him as someone who is psychologically weak enough to let himself become overrun with irrational fear. Consequently, much of the film's success depends on whether the viewer is able to convincingly accept Bogart as capable of such mental instability. Not surprisingly, the film is more divisive than Bogart's other acclaimed works, since it was a daring departure away from the traditional Hollywood narrative structured around the formation of the romantic couple.

Publicity still from *Treasure of the Sierra Madre*

The final film Bogart appeared in with Warner Brothers was *Key Largo* (1948), another film directed by John Huston. He played Frank McCloud, who had been a Major in World War Two. McCloud arrives at the Hotel Largo in Southern Florida, where he falls in love with Nora Temple (Lauren Bacall), the hotel owner's daughter. Nora's husband died in Italy during World War II, and it is revealed that Frank knew him during the war.

Key Largo is a methodical suspense film in the manner of *The Maltese Falcon*. As the plot unfolds, Frank becomes aware that the other guests in the hotel are affiliated with gangster Johnny Rocco (Edward G. Robinson), who also stays at the hotel but refuses to see anyone. Rocco wishes to return to Cuba, where he had been exiled, and he takes Frank, Nora, and her father hostage and orders Frank to transport him and his associates to the island nation. Ultimately, Frank acquiesces but kills them while traveling on the boat.

Key Largo is very much a post-war film that addresses the horrors of killing (it is ambiguous how many men Frank has killed, but the experience has left him weary), as well as the difficulties associated with losing a spouse in the war. However, the film is also remarkably similar to *The Maltese Falcon* in its slow pacing and casting of Bogart in a role where he is outnumbered by villains whom he ultimately defeats. Additionally, the film serves as a commentary on the fall of the gangster genre, a motif that makes the film feel as though it were made a decade earlier. By defeating Johnny Rocco, who is played by an actor who had dominated Bogart early in his career, Bogart effectively usurps his early gangster roles and turns the tables on the subservient role he had played throughout the 1930s.

Bogart and Bacall in *Key Largo*

In addition to becoming more involved in selecting his film roles, Bogart also started his own production company, called Santana Productions. Bogart's decision was met with hostility by Jack Warner; after all, the late 1940s and the 1950s were a difficult time for Hollywood studios because the emergence of television limited the box office totals and fewer major stars were willing to attach themselves to studios. For Bogart though, the idea of operating his own production company was understandably appealing. For years, he had served as a cog in the Warner Brothers machine, taking on many roles he didn't care about. Starting Santana Productions was also in line with the independent-minded characters he portrayed.

During the late 1940s, Bogart also became more politically active. He had always shunned the conservative politics of his parents, even after becoming incredibly rich himself, and the liberal ideology prevalent in Hollywood at the time cohered with his own views. Humphrey advocated on behalf of his colleagues in defense against the House Committee on Un-American Activities, which grew powerful during the Red Scare in the 1950s. At the same time, Bogart was quick to distance himself from the Hollywood Ten, a move that was instrumental in preserving his good name within the industry. He wrote an article for *Photoplay* in which he took pains to point out, "I'm no communist."

The late 1940s also saw Bogart become a father for the first time. In 1949, Bacall gave birth to Stephen Humphrey Bogart. In 1952, they would have a daughter, Leslie Howard, who was named after Bogart's co-star in *The Petrified Forest*. By the standards of the time period, he was particularly old to raise children, and the decision to start a family reflects his satisfaction with his marriage and position of security within the film industry.

Chapter 5: Final Years

"When I chose to be an actor I knew I'd be working in the spotlight. I also knew that the higher a monkey climbs the more you can see of his tail. So I keep my sense of humor and go right on leading my life and enjoying it. I wouldn't trade places with anybody." – Humphrey Bogart

In 1949, Bogart's first films from Santana Productions were released: *Knock on Any Door* (1949) and *Tokyo Joe* (1949). They were followed in 1950 with *Chain Lightning* (1950). These were all relatively unremarkable films, but *Knock on Any Door* put Bogart into contact with Nicholas Ray, a precocious young director who blended the punchy style of John Huston with more expressive formal techniques. Huston was an "actor's director" who favored a motionless camera, while Ray was fond of experimenting with camera angles, heights, and, in his later films, color. Satisfied with the experience of *Knock on Any Door*, Bogart's would again appear in a film directed by Ray, and the film, *In a Lonely Place*, stands as one of his most renowned performances. Bogart's character, Dixon Steele, is an alcoholic writer with a tendency toward acting abusive. He is accused of committing a murder he did not commit, but his erratic behavior draws suspicion from those around him, including his girlfriend. The film juxtaposes scenes in which Steele behaves endearingly with those in which he is abusive. Even though he is eventually exonerated from the crime, his behavior ultimately ruins his relationship.

In a Lonely Place harkens back to the pre-Bacall films in that the film does not end with romantic union. Instead, the film explores the effects of a violent temper both professionally (affecting Steele's productivity as a writer) and personally (he cannot sustain a relationship.) Bogart's character resonates as someone with a utopian desire to escape the constraints of his own paranoia and the conflicts (most notably, the murder accusation that has been leveled towards him) that are imposed on him from the outside world. It sounds somewhat autobiographical too, something actress Louise Brooks picked up on in noting, "[H]e played one fascinatingly complex character…in a film whose title perfectly defined Humphrey's own isolation among people. *In a Lonely Place* gave him a role that he could play with complexity because the film character's, the screenwriter's, pride in his art, his selfishness, his drunkenness, his lack of energy, stabbed with lightning strokes of violence, were shared equally by the real Bogart."

The duality between Bogart's calm and angry temperaments in the film corresponds with Richard Schickel's belief that beneath his gruff façade, Bogart always had a romantic side that was underexplored in his films. Schickel wrote, "In many of these pictures he was woefully miscast as a 'tough guy,' rather than what he was—a romantic hiding his true nature under a gruff and sardonic shell." Certainly, the dichotomy that Schickel sees between the hardened, tough individual and the sweet romantic is on display with *In a Lonely Place*, but it is ultimately Bogart's violent side that overcomes him in the film.

Still photo from *In a Lonely Place*

After *In a Lonely Place*, Bogart teamed up with John Huston one last time, in a film that was not produced by Santana Productions but instead by United Artists, a studio that had been founded roughly three decades before by a group of actors that included Charlie Chaplin. The ambitious film, *The African Queen* (1951), was the first Technicolor film in which Bogart appeared and featured him alongside Katherine Hepburn. The plot involved sinking a German gunboat on the rivers of German-controlled East Africa during World War I. Bogart plays Canadian Charlie Allnut, while Hepburn's character is Rose Sayer, a British missionary. Over the course of the film, they become romantic while also managing to sink the German boat through a plot engineered by Rose.

More than *In a Lonely Place*, *The African Queen* conveys Bogart's romantic side. In fact, the plot line is based around Charlie shedding his tough exterior. By collectively sinking the German boat, the film displays the romantic belief that love between two people can solve any obstacle. The film builds on the romantic side of Bogart that had emerged with through *In a Lonely Place*. Hepburn and Bogart were an interesting pairing too, since she had spent much of her career appearing in screwball comedy films and he had acted in gangster films. They were thus equals and opposites at the same time, two individuals who finally united at a time in which they were beginning to grow old in front of the camera. Consequently, *The African Queen* contains an unusual balance between being an action film on the one hand (shot on location in Africa), while also a sentimental romance between two aging stars.

Hepburn and Bogart in *The African Queen*

The African Queen was a major success for Bogart, and he was awarded his first Academy Award for that performance. However, the film's production was exhaustive and took its toll on the actors. The crew lived on canned food and became ravaged by disease. Hepburn had serious difficulties with the conditions. Nevertheless, the setting on the water rekindled Bogart's love for boats, and he bought a large boat upon returning to the United States. The boat immediately became an integral part of his lifestyle, and he went on short trips nearly every day, balancing work with play in his own singular style.

After *The African Queen*, the next major film in which Bogart appeared was *The Barefoot Contessa*, directed by Joseph Mankiewicz and co-starring Ava Gardner. The film built on the autobiographical bent of *In a Lonely Place*, again casting Humphrey as an artist. He plays Harry Dawes, a film writer and director who works for an oppressive producer. Dawes directs Maria (played by Gardner), and the conflict involves Maria's discontent with being pregnant. In the end, the film is a tragedy, and Dawes is unable to prevent Maria from being killed. As with *In a Lonely Place*, Bogart is an unlikely choice to play the part of an artist. After all, it is difficult to envision Sam Spade or Philip Marlowe watching a movie, let alone writing or directing one. Even so, it is also true that even in his "tough guy" roles, Bogart has a dignified face and an articulate manner of speaking. Critic Stefan Kanfer noted that no matter how far he tried to dissociate himself from his parents, Bogart was never able to full cast aside vestiges of his bourgeois upbringing. He wrote:

> "For all his rebellions against Maud and Belmont, for all his drunken sprees and surly postures, Humphrey could not escape the central fact of his life. He was the scion of straightlaced parents whose roots were in another time. Their

customs and attitudes may have become outmoded, but they were deeply ingrained in their son no matter how hard he tried to escape them. They showed in his upright carriage and in his careful manner of speaking, in his courtesy to women and his frank dealing with men."

In many respects, Bogart was the quintessential modern hero, exhibiting a sometimes precarious balance between desirable and detrimental qualities. However, roles such as *The Barefoot Contessa* attest to the validity of Kanfer's claim. While he still assumes the world-weary feel of his earlier films, he also exudes an eloquence that recalls his privileged upbringing.

Also in 1954, Bogart appeared in the big-budget film *The Caine Mutiny*. In the film, which was Bogart's last major box-office success, he plays Lieutenant Commander Phillip Queeg, a disciplinarian who takes control over the eponymous World War II minesweeper. Queeg's harsh conduct forms the basis for the narrative's conflict, which centers on whether he is insane. Despite the obvious plot differences, Bogart's performance resembles that of *In a Lonely Place* through the instances of unrestrained (and psychotic) rage. Again, the film eschews the romantic grouping characteristic of classical Hollywood narration, as Bogart is relegated to a psychologically disturbed role that gestures to his early gangster performances for Warner Brothers. Still, it is worth noting that Bogart had eagerly sought out the role, demonstrating how he preferred performances that were psychologically unsettling and deviated from the standards for a Hollywood leading man.

The final two years of Bogart's career did not contain any legendary performances. In 1955, he sold his stake in Santana Productions for over $1 million, and he began to develop an even higher profile social life, something largely attributable to Bacall's more outgoing nature. Bogart and Bacall were founding members of the Rat Pack along with Frank Sinatra and a select group of other entertainers. The group would rise to fame after Bogart's death, highlighted by the film *Ocean's Eleven* (1960), and they developed a legacy of hard drinking and easy living.

Dean Martin and Frank Sinatra were both part of the Rat Pack

Bogart's last film was *The Harder They Fall* (1956), directed by Mark Robson. A notable director in his own right, Robson specialized in social realist films during the 1940s, and his style would have been an ideal match for a younger Bogart. In *The Harder They Fall*, Humphrey plays Eddie Willis, an impoverished sportswriter who becomes involved in fixing boxing matches and eventually becomes ashamed and publicizes the seedy injustices of the sports gambling industry.

The Harder They Fall was particularly difficult for Bogart, as he had become quite ill by the time the film was made. Always a heavy bourbon drinker and cigarette smoker, he developed cancer of the esophagus, the effects of which were worsened by the fact that he refused to see a doctor until January of 1956. By this point, the cancer had rapidly progressed, and Bogart's health went into swift decline. In March 1956, he had his esophagus, two lymph nodes, and a rib removed.

Unable to make any more films, his life and career ended in concert. Instead of making any additional films during that year, 1956 was spent saying farewells to his family and acquaintances. He took his poor health in stride, and even had his dumbwaiter custom designed so that he could ride in a wheelchair up and down to get around: "Put me in the dumbwaiter and I'll ride down to the first floor in style."

Bogart lasted for one year after his diagnosis, finally passing away on January 14, 1957. By then, his 57 year old body had withered to just 80 pounds. Huston gave the eulogy at Bogart's family and said:

> "Bogie's hospitality went far beyond food and drink. He fed a guest's spirit as was well as his body, plied him with good will until he became drunk in the heart as well as his legs...Himself, he never took too seriously—his work most seriously. He regarded the somewhat gaudy figure of Bogart, the star, with an amused cynicism; Bogart, the actor, he held in deep respect...In each of the fountains at Versailles there is a pike which keeps all the carp active; otherwise they would grow overfat and die. Bogie took rare delight in performing a similar duty in the fountains of Hollywood. Yet his victims seldom bore him any malice, and when they did, not for long. His shafts were fashioned only to stick into the outer layer of complacency, and not to penetrate through to the regions of the spirit where real injuries are done...He is quite irreplaceable. There will never be another like him."

Bogart died a premature death, just three years after being nominated for an Academy Award in *The Caine Mutiny*, but it is worth considering whether his career would have remained successful. By the mid-1950s, Bogart's tough, unsentimental acting style was becoming outdated by a more sensitive acting style, a development attributable to the popularity of the Actors Studio headed by Lee Strasberg in New York City. While Bogart displayed little emotion, actors like Marlon Brando and James Dean won audiences over with sweeping portrayals of sensitive, disturbed characters. Had Bogart's career continued, he almost certainly would have continued to find consistent employment, but it is likely that his days as a leading man were coming to an end, regardless of his cancer.

Bogart's legacy has only grown in size since his death, and today it extends well beyond his iconic character type and roles in films like *The Maltese Falcon*, *Casablanca*, and *Key Largo*. While those movies inextricably linked with the crime genre as a whole, Bogart's subsequent characters (from the 1940s onward) behaved with honor but also an understanding that traditional views of morality were inadequate in the context of modern life. This helped solidify Bogart as an iconic modern hero who not only behaves virtuously but does so in an approachable, psychologically realistic manner that understands the difficulties of life. In his pseudo-obituary on Bogart, Andre Bazin describes Bogart thusly: "Humphrey Bogart was a modern hero. The period film—the historical romance or pirate story—didn't suit him. He was the starter at the race, the man who had a revolver with only one bullet, the guy in the felt hat that he could flick a finger with to express anger or gaiety." This description in particular, treating anger and joy as twin emotions, reflects the monumental effect that he had on audiences.

In a similar vein, Bogart and his roles continue to be relevant today because of the individualistic nature that his characters had. As actor Rod Steiger put it, "Bogart has endured because in our society the family unit has gone to pieces. And here you had a guy about whom there was no doubt. There is no doubt that he is the leader. There is no doubt that he is the strong one. There is no doubt with this man that he can handle himself, that he can protect the family. This is all unconscious, but with Bogart you are secure, you never doubt that he will take care of things." This also extended to the man himself, as friend and biographer Nathaniel Benchley wrote of him, "He achieved class through his integrity and his devotion to what he thought was right. He believed in being direct, simple, and honest, all on his own terms, and this ruffled some people and endeared him to others."

Ultimately, Bogart showed people how to respond in a modern way to a modern world, and that even an ordinary man can navigate the challenges of life.

Bibliography

Bazin, Andre. "A Portrait of Humphrey Bogart." *The Films of My Life*. Cambridge: Da Capo Press, 1994.

Brooks, Louise. "Humphrey & Bogey." *Sight and Sound* 36.1 (Winter 1967). Accessed from http://www.psykickgirl.com/lulu/bogey.html.

Dyer, Richard. *Stars*. London: BFI, 1986.

Eco, Umberto. "Casablanca, or, The Cliches are Having a Ball," *Signs of Life in the U.S.A.: Readings on Popular Culture for Writers*, Eds. Sonia Maasik and Jack Solomon, Boston: Bedford Books, 1994, 260-264.

Farber, Manny. *Farber on Film: The Complete Film Writings of Manny Farber*. Ed. Robert Polito. New York: Library of America, 2009.

Gledhill, Christina. "Signs of Melodrama." *Stardom: Industry of Desire*. Ed. Christine Gledhill. New York: Routledge Press, 1991.

Kael, Pauline. "About Comic-Strip Style, from a Sense of Disproportion." *For Keeps: 30 Years at the Movies*. 103-105.

Kanfer, Stefan. *Tough Without a Gun: The Extraordinary Life and Afterlife of Humphrey Bogart*. New York: Random House, 2011.

McArthur, Colin. *Underworld, USA*. London: Secker & Warburg, 1972.

Meyers, Jeffrey. *Bogart: A Life in Hollywood*. London: Deutsch, 1997.

Porter, Darwin. *The Secret Life of Humphrey Bogart: The Early Years (1899-1931)*. New York: Blood Moon Productions, 2003.

Schickel, Richard. *Bogie: A Celebration of the Life and Films of Humphrey Bogart*. London: Aurum Press Ltd., 2006.

Thomson, David. *Humphrey Bogart*. New York: Faber and Faber, 2009.

James Cagney

Chapter 1: From Street to Stage

"It was just everyday living. With me, it was fighting, more fighting, and more fighting. Life then was simply the way it was: ordinary, not bad, not good, just regular. No stress, no strain. Of course, no one had much of anything but we didn't know that we were poor." – James Cagney

On July 17, 1899, James Cagney was born on the tough streets of the Lower East Side of Manhattan, and at the time his family was so poor that they didn't bother keeping careful records of family births and addresses, so the actual location of his birthplace remains a mystery. His father, James Francis Cagney, worked any job he could find and was, at one time or another, a bartender, a boxer and (at the time of his second son's birth) a telegraphist. Cagney's mother, Carolyn, was a first generation American with roots in Ireland and Norway, and it was from her that Cagney inherited his red hair, blue eyes and hot temper.

Cagney was the second of seven children, but two of Cagney's siblings died within months of their birth, which the family attributed to their poverty. As Cagney put it in his own autobiography, there was almost a third: "I was a very sick infant. My mother, only 20 – a mere child herself – was terribly worried, of course. What bothered her most, next to my possible demise, was the fact that I hadn't been baptized. As a good Catholic, she felt that if I were to die before I was given a proper name, I'd never be allowed into heaven. She bemoaned this again and again to her brother: 'He hasn't got the name – he has to have a name!' Now, my uncle was a pretty rough Irishman. He humored her for a while, but Mom continued to cry the house down about my lack of identity. Finally he turned on her and said, 'Carrie, for God's sake, shut up! Stop your crying and call the kid Ikey!" At that time, the Lower East side was characterized more than anything else by its diversity, ensuring Cagney grew up surrounded by people who had come to America from all over the world. He would later be grateful for this type of upbringing, noting, "The polyglot nature of my neighborhood is the basic reason why all my life I've had such an appreciation and understanding for dialects. I ought to – I was surrounded by them. Indeed, I was 22 before I ever heard an elderly man who spoke without an accent…"

Like most living in the heart of New York City at that time, the young boy always had a job. At one time, it was as an office boy for the *New York Sun* making $5 a week, all of which he gave to his mother. Later, he worked at the New York Public Library for $12.50 a month. He also played semi-pro baseball and he was so good at amateur boxing that he once finished runner-up for the lightweight boxing title in New York State. He wanted to turn professional, but his mother warned him he would have to beat her first, so he soon gave up the idea. Cagney later recounted his time working as a young kid positively, explaining, "It was good for me. I feel sorry for the kid who has too cushy a time of it. Suddenly he has to come face-to-face with the realities of life without any mama or papa to do his thinking for him."

After it was clear he wasn't going to be a boxer, Jimmy next turned to a less suitable but more lucrative line of work: serving as a maître d' at an upscale tea room. His job at the tea room may seem strange, considering Cagney's tough guy image, but he was certainly more rounded than the average street tough. In addition to boxing and playing baseball, he also took tap dancing lessons, and friends that knew him as a young man recall him as "Cellar Door Cagney" thanks to the knack he had for dancing up the side of slanted cellar doors.

Nor was young Jimmy Cagney all brawn and no brain. After graduating from Stuyvesant High School in 1918, Cagney enrolled in Columbia University as an art major, but by this time, the United States had entered World War I. Assuming that the war would go on for a number of years, and already having an ear for German gained as a child, Cagney also decided to major in the language. This immediately benefited him when it came to joining the Student Army Training Corps, a predecessor of the Army ROTC, and Cagney might have gone on to a career in the military had fate not intervened. The war ended in November 1918, and an influenza pandemic swept through the world, taking the life of his father and leaving his mother a young widow pregnant with her seventh child. This sudden turn of events forced Cagney to drop out of school and move home to help make ends meet.

Thankfully, Jimmy Cagney had some sort of photographic memory, which not only helped him excel in school but also opened the door for his acting career. Like so many other would-be actors, his interest in performing began with the movies. Cagney's aunt lived in Brooklyn near the Vitagraph Studios, and while visiting her, Cagney would hang over the edge of the fence surrounding the studios and watch movies being filmed, especially those involving his favorite actor, John Bunny.

John Bunny

Eventually, Jimmy would follow his older brother Henry into the amateur dramatic club at the Lenox Hill Neighborhood House, where he worked primarily behind the scenes as a stagehand. At the time, the younger Cagney had no interest in acting, but that all changed one night when Harry became too ill to carry on with his part. The director, Florence James, called on Jimmy to take his brother's place, and because of his excellent memory, Jimmy had no problems learning the script. He went on stage that night with the lines memorized and mimicked his brother's acting movements, which he had remembered from watching rehearsals. Naturally, the applause from the audience proved to be a thrill for him and left him wanting more.

Chapter 2: The Boxer Who Danced

"You know, the period of World War I and the Roaring Twenties were really just about the same as today. You worked, and you made a living if you could, and you tried to make the best of things. For an actor or a dancer, it was no different then than today. It was a struggle." – James Cagney

Jimmy might have been bitten by the acting bug, but playing bit parts in dramatic companies was not going to pay the bills, so he also got a full-time job at Wanamaker's Department Store in 1919. Undeterred, he was still working there when he auditioned for a small part in *Every Sailor*, a war time musical with a chorus made up of service men dressed as women. He later explained the unusual nature of this first part: "And that is how I began to learn dancing, as a chorus girl. I faked it to begin with. I would stand in the entrance, catch the real dancers, and steal their steps. Thereafter, in all the dancing shows and acts I did, I learned by watching." While it would certainly surprise many to hear that the classic Hollywood tough guy played his first part in drag, it didn't faze Cagney at all because when he was acting, "I am not myself. I am not that fellow, Jim Cagney, at all. I certainly lost all consciousness of him when I put on skirts, wigs, make-up, powder, feathers and bangles." It certainly didn't hurt that they were paying Cagney $35 a week, which he considered "a mountain of money for me in those worrisome days."

Though Carrie was proud of her second son's success, she still wanted him to return to college and get a degree. He refused to go back, but he did leave the department store and take a position as a runner for a local Broad Street brokerage house, and in his off time, he continued to audition, eventually getting a part in the chorus of *Pitter Patter*. He was paid over $50 a week, but he sent $40 of it to his mother. More accustomed to hard work than the life of an actor, Cagney also made additional money by working as a dresser and carrying luggage for the other actors. The show proved to be Cagney's first part in vaudeville.

While working on the ticker counter, Cagney met Frances Willard "Billie" Vernon, a 16-year-old member of the female chorus line, and they soon fell in love and married in 1922. They then moved into a sort of early style of commune called Free Acres that was established in Berkeley Heights, New Jersey. Cagney and his wife would tour together with an act called "Vernon & Ide", and later, he would replace Archie Leach, of the Parker, Brandon and Leach act. The name Archie Leach doesn't mean much to anyone anymore because Leach later changed his name to Cary Grant.

Cary Grant

Cagney and his wife with actors Jack Oakie and Joan Marsh

In 1924, Vernon and Cagney moved across the country to Hawthorne, California to try to break into the movies, even though they were so poor at that time that they had to borrow the train fare from a friend who was also an aspiring actor. At first, Cagney tried to support himself and his wife by teaching dancing, but perhaps not surprisingly, there were already plenty of dance schools near them and thus not enough clients. Cagney was unable to make ends meet, forcing the couple to give up on their dream of making it out West. They borrowed more money to move back to New York. These were obviously hard times, and Jimmy never forgot them, or what it took for them to make it through. More than 50 years later, he would give his wife the credit, saying "the rock solid honesty and the sterling character of this little gal made it possible our going comparatively unscathed through the years when we were in dire straits. And when I say dire straits, I mean 'dire' and I mean 'straits.' It was rough. At times no food in the larder, big holes in the shoes. When I didn't have a penny, she was out working. Life seemed just a never ending sequence of damned dingy, badly furnished rooms with a one burner plate. There were many times when I was sorely tried and decided to get out of the acting business, to go out and get any kind of job that would bring in the weekly paycheck. But every time I mentioned it, my Bill told me with pleasant firmness, no."

Fortunately, Cagney fared better on the stage than he did in the movies. In 1925, he was cast as a tough guy in the play *Outside Looking In*, and his work in that production earned him a far more comfortable living at $200 a week. Since he had no experience doing dramatic acting, Cagney later admitted he thought he got the part because his hair was redder than that of the other performer he was competing against, but regardless, the play was popular and garnered Cagney a number of positive reviews. One critic in *Life* magazine noted, "Mr. Cagney, in a less spectacular role makes a few minutes silence during his mock-trial scene something that many a more established actor might watch with profit". Burns Mantle, a stage critic who founded and wrote for *Best Plays*, claimed *Outside Looking In* "contained the most honest acting now to be seen in New York."

However, Cagney faced another major setback in 1926, when he was promised but then lost a part in George Abbott's Broadway. Believing that they would be sailing to England to perform the show in London's West End, Jimmy and Billie had their luggage loaded on to a ship and had given up the lease on their apartment, but the day before they were to leave, Cagney was told that he no longer had the part. Cagney's wife later recalled that after this turn of events, "Jimmy said that it was all over. He made up his mind that he would get a job doing something else."

That something else turned out to be something familiar. To make ends meet, Cagney tried his hand again at teaching dance, and this time, his students were fellow professionals, so he was able to make more money. More importantly, he was also able to hear about new plays opening, which is how he secured a role in *Women Go on Forever*. For four months, Cagney taught dance all day, and danced across the stage all night. By the time the play ended, he was both physically and mentally exhausted.

The following year, Cagney was cast in *Grand Street Follies of 1928*, and this time, he was also made the choreographer. The Follies were a hit, which led to the reprisal of the show the following year as the aptly named *Grand Street Follies of 1929*. In vaudeville, as in life, Cagney soon learned that nothing succeeds like success; his successful roles in the Follies led to a part in *Maggie the Magnificent*. Though the critics didn't much care for the play, they praised Cagney's performance, and Cagney praised director George Kelly for his professionalism: "On *Maggie the Magnificent*'s first day of rehearsal, he said to us, 'Now, boys and girls, we have hired you because we know you were experienced. I will benefit of all that experience. We think you know your business. Anything that occurs to you, please let me know – because I can't think of everything. So – if you would do me the favor of speaking up? All right now, let's get to work.' Naturally, with such a complete professional in control, there was no need for us to give him anything." Cagney also said he learned "what a director was for and what a director could do. They were directors who could play all the parts in the play better than the actors cast for them."

Chapter 3: The Public Enemy Becomes a Public Hero

"Though I soon became typecast in Hollywood as a gangster and hoodlum, I was originally a dancer, an Irish hoofer, trained in vaudeville tap dance. I always leapt at the opportunity to dance films later on." – James Cagney

Following *Maggie the Magnificent*, Cagney and his co-star Joan Blondell were cast in a new play called *Penny Arcade*. As with the previous play, the critics did not like *Penny Arcade*, but they loved Cagney and Blondell, and when Al Jolson saw the couple's talent, he bought the rights to the play for $20,000 and then turned around and sold the play to Warner Bros., with the caveat that they would hire Cagney and Blondell to re-create their parts on screen. Warner Bros. cast the two, giving Cagney a three week contract for $1500 to play tough guy Harry Delano, and this type of part would prove to be his bread and butter for the rest of his career. Despite the fact it was his first film, Cagney refused to be cowed into doing stuff he didn't like, including a scene he wouldn't shoot: "There was a line in the show where I was supposed to be crying on my mother's breast...'I'm your baby, ain't I?' I refused to say it. Adolfi said 'I'm going to tell Zanuck.' I said 'I don't give a s*** what you tell him, I'm not going to say that line.'" By holding firm, Cagney had the line removed from the script.

Joan Blondell

The film adaptation of *Penny Arcade*, titled *Sinners' Holiday*, was released in 1930, but Cagney's on screen career began not so much with a bang but with a whimper. The studio liked him, but they weren't sure how much they liked him. Thus, when the shooting ended, Warner offered him a seven-year contract for salary of $400 a week, but the studio added an unusual stipulation that specified it could drop him at the end of any 40 week period. In other words, Cagney could find himself out of work after any 40 week period, but since he had no better offers and still needed to support his family, he took the contract. When looking at Cagney's decision sign with Warner Bros., it's essential to keep in mind his background. $400 a week was a substantial amount of money for a family that had grown up broke, and by this time, the stock market had crashed and many Americans had no work at all. At the time, getting paid $400 a week to stand in front of the camera was easy money in his mind, though he would soon change his mind.

Cagney's next picture was *Doorway to Hell*, and it was followed by several other gangster films, including *Little Caesar*, in which he played opposite Edward G Robinson for the first time. Over the next few years, these two men would come to define what it meant to be a gangster in a Hollywood film, but ultimately, Cagney's big break became in 1931 when he was cast in *The Public Enemy*. The very nature of the casting for that film is the stuff of Hollywood legend, as Cagney would later recall: "Then came *The Public Enemy*. The story is about two street pals – one soft-spoken, the other a really tough little article. For some incredible reason, I was cast as the quiet one; and Eddie Woods, a fine actor but a boy of genial background, well-spoken and well-educated, became the tough guy. Fortunately, Bill Wellman, the director, had seen *Doorway to Hell*, and he quickly became aware of the obvious casting error. He knew at once that I can project that direct gutter quality, so Eddie and I switched roles after Wellman made an issue of it with Darryl Zanuck."

Wellman clearly made the right decision, because *The Public Enemy* soon became one of the first films to ever gross more than $1 million. Not only did the public love the movie, the critics loved it. A reviewer in the *New York Herald* said that Cagney's performance was "the most ruthless, unsentimental appraisal of the meanness of a petty killer the cinema has yet devised." Some critics have cited the film as changing the way that the public would perceive good guys versus bad guys, asserting that Cagney's portrayal of Tom Powers as a murderer with a heart of gold introduced the genre to Hollywood. However, Cagney always disagreed, pointing instead to Clark Gable in *Night Nurse* as being the first "good bad guy".

The movie attempted to be so realistic that Cagney was actually punched in the face in one scene, and another called for him to duck from live gunfire, but the most famous scene in the movie comes when Cagney's character angrily picks up half of a grapefruit and shoves it into his girlfriend's (played by Mae Clarke) face. The shocking nature of the scene, and the surprise on Clarke's face, led many to assume that it was an impromptu move on either Cagney's part of the director's part, and that Clarke wasn't told what was coming her way. For her part, Clarke claimed that she knew the grapefruit was coming, but that she had been told it wouldn't actually be included in the movie itself: "I'm sorry I ever agreed to do the grapefruit bit. I never dreamed it would be shown in the movie. Director Bill Wellman thought of the idea suddenly. It wasn't even written into the script." Even today, movie experts refer to it as one of the most significant moments in film history, and naturally, Cagney had his own take on the issue: "When Mae Clarke and I played the grapefruit scene, we had no idea that it would create such a stir...I was not to hear the end of that little episode for years. Invariably whenever I went into a restaurant, there was always some wag having the waiter bring me a tray of grapefruit. It got to be awfully tiresome, although it never stopped me from eating it in the proper amount at the proper time."

Cagney was glad to have work, and he appreciated the money he was making, but he was still the scrappy tough guy from the Lower East Side who refused to be pushed around by anyone. For instance, when Douglas Fairbanks, Jr. organized a charity drive, the studio insisted that every actor participate, but Cagney refused, saying that while he was glad to donate to charity, he would not be forced to do it. This incident and subsequent others would eventually earn him the title "The Professional Againster" in Hollywood.

While shooting *The Public Enemy*, Cagney was also working with Edward Robinson on *Smart Money*. Warner liked the way the two men interacted on screen, so the studio wanted them to get back together in another film as soon as possible. In spite of the fact that he had never hit a woman in real life, Cagney was once again called upon to assault his leading lady in *Smart Money*. This time, he had to slap his co-star, Evelyn Knapp. However, things were changing in Hollywood at the beginning of the 1930s, as motion pictures, once considered a novelty, were becoming more mainstream in American society. With that came an outcry from conservative Americans and religious groups to limit the amount of sex and violence in pictures. Needless to say, they did not appreciate films in which men assaulted women, and they also didn't like criminals being portrayed as having redeeming qualities. Warner decided to take Cagney's career in another direction by casting him with Joan Blondell in a comedy, *Blonde Crazy*, but this new direction wouldn't last long.

Chapter 4: Working For and Against Warner Bros.

"There were many tough guys to play in the scripts that Warner kept assigning me. Each of my subsequent roles in the hoodlum genre offered the opportunity to inject something new, which I always tried to do. One could be funny, and the next one flat. Some roles were mean, and others were meaner." – James Cagney

The Public Enemy was so popular that movie theaters were running the movie 24 hours a day just to keep up with demand; in fact, one legendary anecdote about the movie related by Cagney is that Joan Blondell's ex-husband figured out the times the grapefruit scene would be on and would duck into the theater to catch it as often as possible. Given the movie's popularity, Cagney realized that he was bringing in a lot of money for Warner Bros. but was not being paid as much as many of the other actors whose films were not doing as well. He approached the executives at the company and demanded a raise, and when they refused and also insisted that he spend his extra time promoting other films, Cagney quit, turned his apartment in Hollywood over to his brother Bill, and moved back to New York. He would describe his rationale for this move: "The trouble surfaced when I realized that there were roughly two classes of stars at Warner's: those getting $125,000 a picture – and yours sincerely, who was getting all of $400 a week. That $400 soon stopped because I walked."

While it was obviously a risky decision, it was also a wise one, because the popularity of *The Public Enemy* and *Blonde Crazy* had the public clamoring to see more of him. While Jimmy was gone, his brother was able to persuade Warner to renew his contract and pay him $1000 a week, after which Cagney returned to Hollywood and began working on *Taxi*. This film marked both a first and a last in his career. The first was his dancing, as he performed an excellent number on screen for the first time. The last was getting shot at with live ammunition. At the time, studios regularly shot at their actors with live rounds because blanks were considered too expensive, and Cagney had taken it for granted that it was part of the job. However, during the filming of *Taxi*, something happened that changed his mind: "…one of the machine-gun bullets hit the head of one of the spikes holding the backing planks together. It ricocheted and went tearing through the set, smacked through a sound booth, ripped across the stage, hit a clothes tree, and dropped into the pocket of someone's coat." From that point forward, Cagney refused to put himself in the line of fire, and that decision may have saved his life on the set of *Angels with Dirty Faces* because an errant bullet passed through the place where he would have otherwise been standing.

The film *Taxi* also contains one of the most misquoted lines in movie history. At one point in time, Cagney yells at his enemy, "Come out and take it, you dirty, yellow-bellied rat, or I'll give it to you through the door!" For some reason, this line began to be quoted all over the nation as, "MMMmmm, you dirty rat!" To this day, impressionists still use it when impersonating Cagney.

Warner may have thought that they had won the battle with Cagney over his salary, but they were wrong. Cagney returned to Hollywood for $1000 a week, but he believed that his work was worth $4000 a week, which is what Edward G. Robinson and other actors of the era were making. Cagney again demanded a raise and again threatened to quit if he did not get it, but this time, the studio called his bluff and suspended him. Cagney responded that if that was their attitude, he would quit acting altogether and return to Columbia University to become a doctor. Finally, after six months of wrestling, Frank Capra was able to persuade Cagney to accept $3000 per week, along with top billing and the assurance that he would have to film no more than four movies a year. This success would lead to Cagney becoming one of the leading members of the Screen Actors Guild when it was founded in 1933.

1933 and 1934 had Cagney making multiple movies for Warner Bros., and as is usually the case, some were better received than others. *Footlight Parade* was particularly popular, and Cagney enjoyed making it because it allowed him to sing and dance on stage again. The dance sequences, choreographed by the famous Busby Berkeley, are considered some of the best of the era. Cagney's other favorite movie of that time was *Here Comes the Navy*, not so much because of the quality of the film but because he got to work with Pat O'Brien, who would become one of his best friends. Ironically, the movie was filmed aboard the USS *Arizona*, several years before it would be sunk by the Japanese at Pearl Harbor.

Cagney and Blondell in *Footlight Parade*

Cagney and Gloria Stuart in *Here Comes the Navy*

By 1935, Cagney was considered one of the 10 biggest moneymakers in Hollywood, but when asked if this was the big moment when he realized he was a star, he replied with his usual honesty: "Nothing of the sort! I never gave it a thought, never thought of it at all. Whatever was going on in my Hollywood life I regarded as completely transitory. I looked on it only as doing a job, and that job happened to work out. And the answer to all this is, where did I go nights? I sure wasn't going around picking up the kudos – or the kiddos. I just stayed home."

Cagney finally got to be on the other side of the cops and robbers game in *G-Men*, this time playing an FBI agent tracking down a wanted criminal. After that, he made his first and only foray into Shakespeare by portraying Nick Bottom in *A Midsummer's Night's Dream*. Needless to say, he would not try such a role again.

Instead, Cagney next made a third film with Pat O'Brien, this one called *Ceiling Zero*, but in this film, Warner again challenged Cagney's contract. First, they listed O'Brien above him in the credits, a clear violation of his top billing clause, and the company had already pushed Cagney by having him make five movies in 1934, another violation. He had let this pass, but the billing issue proved to be the final straw. He sued the studio for breach of contract, and after again leaving Bill to handle his professional and business matters, he returned to New York. When looking at his contract battle with Warner, particularly his preference to renegotiate over and over again, it may seem that Cagney was stubbornly insistent on having his way at all costs, but he cast his actions in a different light: "Top billing is an entitlement that means money in the bank, and I was protecting my entitlement. I walked out because I depended on the studio heads to keep their word on this, that, or other promise, and when the promise was not kept, my only recourse was to deprive them of my services. I'd go back east and stay on my farm until I had some kind of understanding. I'm glad to say I never walked out in the middle of a picture, the usual procedure when an actor wanted a raise."

Back in New York, Cagney began shopping around for property outside the city and claiming that he would just settle down to farm. Though he grew up in the city, Cagney had been interested in farming ever since his mother took him to hear a talk on soil conservation when he was a young man. Thus, while he was off from work, he purchased his first farm. Located on Martha's Vineyard, it consisted of 100 acres of bucolic quiet, but his wife didn't care for the place at first; Billie was concerned about the money and work it would take to make the deteriorated old house and out buildings habitable. Jimmy persisted, however, and she soon came to love it too. For his part, Carney maintained that the Vineyard "represented for me the place where I could always go to find freedom and peace…"

Of course, the Cagney's would have to work hard to maintain their peace, especially after Jimmy's fans learned where they lived. In order to avoid multiple strangers showing up at his door, Cagney spread the rumor around the area that he had hired an armed guard to patrol the place. This led to a comical situation when his pal Spencer Tracy came to visit. Tracy's cabbie would not pull up on to the property, explaining to him "I hear they shoot!" Thus, Tracy had to walk up the dirt road on foot to get to the house.

Jimmy Cagney the actor might have disappeared altogether and been permanently replaced by Jimmy Cagney the gentleman farmer had it not been for Edward L. Alperson, who represented Grand National Films, a new studio that offered Cagney $100,000 per film plus 10% of whatever the movies made. Cagney accepted this deal and returned to Hollywood to make *Great Guy* and *Something to Think About* for Grand National. These movies are unique among his performances of that era in that he plays a more sympathetic "good guy" rather than a criminal, but while his performances were critically acclaimed, the movies themselves were low-budget and looked it. Grand National ran out of money before it could make any more films, and Cagney once more found himself looking for a new project.

Cagney did not have to look for long; he won his case against Warner Bros., setting a new precedent for actors who had formally been bound by the studio system. More than that, the studio actually invited him to return to work for them, this time offering him a contract for $150,000 per film, with a clause guaranteeing that he would have to make no more than two movies each year. He could also choose which pictures he made. Always a family man, Jimmy insisted that his brother Bill be made the assistant producer of any movies he was cast in.

Cagney's victory against Warner Bros. proved to be a triumph in the politics of Hollywood, and it also led him to become involved in other political matters, a decision that would later cause him some problems. In 1936, the specter of war was consuming Europe, with Hitler and the Nazis in Germany and Mussolini rattling his saber in Italy. The world was watching, and though most Americans were still isolationists, Cagney believed that the Nazis needed to be stopped. As a result, he joined the Hollywood anti-Nazi League, unaware that the League was actually a Communist front. This would come back to haunt him later.

In the meantime, Cagney was back working for Warner Bros. After working with Pat O'Brien in *Boy Meets Girl* in 1938, Cagney teamed up with him again in the classic *Angels with Dirty Faces*. Cagney had had his eye on this role for some time and had hoped to make it for Grand National. In it, he stars as recently released gangster Rocky Sullivan, and while trying to track down an old pal who owes him money (played by Humphrey Bogart), Sullivan runs into another old friend, Jerry Connolly. Played by O'Brien, Connolly is now a priest working with at-risk kids, many of whom idolize Rocky. He tries to persuade Sullivan to go straight but fails, and Sullivan ends up being sentenced to the electric chair.

Cagney and O'Brien in *Angels with Dirty Faces*

In the moments leading up to his execution, Connolly visits Sullivan and pleads with him to "turn yellow", so that the kids who have so admired him will lose their respect for him and his criminal ways. Sullivan refuses to humiliate himself and insists that he will walk to the chair like a man. However, at the last moment, he falls to his knees before his executioners and pleads for his life. For years, critics would speculate over whether Sullivan's seeming cowardice at the last minute was a real last ditch attempt to save his life or feigned to appease Connolly, but Cagney would never say: "Through the years I have actually had little kids come up to me on the street and ask, 'Didya' do it for the father?' I think in looking at the film it is virtually impossible to say which course Rocky took – which is just the way I wanted it. I played it with deliberate ambiguity so that the spectator can take his choice. It seems to me it works out fine in either case. You have to decide."

Critics hailed Cagney's performance in *Angels with Dirty Faces* as one of his best, and he received his first Oscar nomination for Best Actor, but he ultimately lost out to Spencer Tracy, who ironically won it for playing a priest in *Boys Town*. However, Cagney did snag the coveted New York Film Critics Circle award for best actor, and it would hardly be his last Academy Award nomination.

By 1939, hard work and a hard-nosed approach to business had made Cagney the studio's highest paid actor. In fact, his annual salary of $350,000 was second only to Cary Grant's in the entire industry. While Warner probably didn't appreciate the route Cagney took to get to that position, the studio also knew it was money well spent. Cagney finished up the year with *The Roaring Twenties*, his last film with Bogart and the last gangster movie he would make for a decade. As usual, he received good reviews, with Graham Greene remarking, "Mr. Cagney, of the bull-calf brow, is as always a superb and witty actor".

Cagney with Bogart and Jeffrey Lynn in *The Roaring Twenties*

The Roaring Twenties marked the end of another era for Cagney, although this time the change was more subtle. As noted earlier, Hollywood was under increasing scrutiny for the moral message of its films, and during the 1930s, most of Cagney's gangster characters were portrayed as having turned to a life of crime because of being raised in abusive and/or poor environments. As the 1940s dawned, public perspective was shifting, and from this time on, large-scale violence was seen as part of a mental illness or, at the very least, a lack of self-control.

Chapter 5: Yankee Doodle Dandy

Cagney in *Yankee Doodle Dandy*

By 1941, Jimmy and Billie Cagney had been married almost 20 years, but they still had no children, so they decided to adopt an infant boy whom they named James Cagney, Jr. A few years later, they would adopt a girl and name her Cathleen. Tragically, while Jimmy and Billie remained close throughout their marriage, they had a difficult relationship with their children. James Jr. died two years before his father following a long period in which the two were estranged, and Cathleen would remain estranged from her father until his death.

Jimmy Cagney is best known for playing gangsters with one notable exception: his portrayal of George M. Cohan in *Yankee Doodle Dandy*. Both critics and Cagney himself believed it was his best role ever, and there are a number of reasons (in addition to Cagney's talent) *Yankee Doodle Dandy* was such a hit. One is that the crew began filming the picture on December 8, 1941, the day after the bombing of Pearl Harbor, so it goes without saying that everyone working on the project was in a state of what one person called "patriotic frenzy." Cagney's co-star, Rosemary DeCamp, noted the cast and crew had a feeling that "they might be sending the last message from the free world" out to the country. At the premiere, the company sold seats for up to $25,000 each, donating the money to the U.S. Treasury in the form of war bonds, and in that one evening they raised almost $6 million for the war effort.

Another factor that made the film a hit involved the parallels between Cohan's and Cagney's lives. Both men got their start in vaudeville, they both struggled hard before finding success, they both were devoted to their families, and they had both been married to the same women for many years, which was no small feat in Hollywood then (or now).

Cohan

Both the public and the critics loved the movie. *Time* wrote, "*Yankee Doodle Dandy* (Warner) is possibly the most genial screen biography ever made. Few films have bestowed such loving care on any hero as this one does on beaming, buoyant, wry-mouthed George M. (for Michael) Cohan. The result is a nostalgic, accurate re-creation of a historic era of U.S. show business." As far as Cagney's performance was concerned, they were equally enthusiastic, noting, "Smart, alert, hard-headed, Cagney is as typically American as Cohan himself... It was a remarkable performance, probably Cagney's best, and it makes Yankee Doodle a dandy." Perhaps the biggest praise came from Cohan himself; when he saw Cagney's performance in the film he exclaimed, "My God, what an act to follow!"

Of course, one of the reasons Cagney succeeded in the role was the very reason he was cast for it: "Psychologically I needed no preparation for Yankee Doodle Dandy, or professionally either. I didn't have to pretend to be a song-and-dance man. I was one…In just about every interview, in most conversations, one question emerges unfailingly: what is my favorite picture?…A discerning critic like Peter Bogdonovich can't understand why I choose *Yankee Doodle Dandy*...The answer is simple...Once a song-and-dance man, always a song-and-dance man. In that brief statement, you have my life story: those few words tells as much about me professionally as there is to tell....Its story abounds in all the elements necessary for a good piece of entertainment. It has solid laughs [and] great music. And how much more meaningful are those patriotic songs today in view of all our current national troubles! *Yankee Doodle Dandy* has lots of reasons to be my favorite picture." When Cagney wrote those words in 1974, the troubles he referred to were very different than those faced at the time of the film's release, but *Yankee Doodle Dandy* stood the test of time. Even today, it remains an American favorite.

Not surprisingly, considering the both the nature of the film and the year in which it was released, *Yankee Doodle Dandy* was nominated for eight Academy Awards. It won three, including Cagney's win for Best Actor. When accepting his award, he remained humble, saying, "I've always maintained that in this business, you're only as good as the other fellow thinks you are. It's nice to know that you people thought I did a good job. And don't forget that it was a good part, too."

Following his success with *Yankee Doodle Dandy*, Cagney teamed up with his brother Bill to create Cagney Productions, and their plan was to make movies themselves and then release them through United Artists. However, Cagney was in no hurry to get back to work; instead, he returned to his farm on Martha's Vineyard to rest up. After that, with the war still ongoing, he joined the United Service Organizations (USO) and began touring military bases and visiting soldiers. At each base, he would recreate scenes from *Yankee Doodle Dandy*, as well as some of his early song and dance work.

In September 1942, Cagney returned to Hollywood and was elected as president of the Screen Actors Guild. The following year, Cagney Productions released its first film, *Johnny Come Lately*, starring Cagney as a newspaperman in the late 19th century. According to Cagney, "...our biggest accomplishment in *Johnny Come Lately* was to establish as one of the hallmarks of Cagney Productions the liberal use of good supporting actors. As Time magazine said about this, 'Bit players who have tried creditably for years to walk in shoes that pinched them show themselves in this picture as the very competent actors they always were. There has seldom been as good a cinematic gallery of U.S. small-town types.'"

Jimmy and his brother took a real chance with *Johnny Come Lately* because most of the larger studios were focusing on making war films, and that's what the American public seemed to want. While the film did receive some positive reviews and made a reasonable amount of money, it was not the type of hit Cagney was used to making. Thus, instead of beginning to work on another film right away, he went on another USO tour, this time to England.

Cagney enjoyed his time in England and worked hard to entertain the troops stationed on military bases there. He often gave multiple performances in a single day of his main act, "The

American Cavalcade of Dance", a history of dance in 20th century America, and finishing with numbers from Yankee Doodle Dandy. The only thing that Cagney wouldn't do was give interviews to reporters covering the tour; when some British reporters approached him one time, he responded, "I'm here to dance a few jigs, sing a few songs, say hello to the boys, and that's all."

When Cagney came home, he quickly got to work on Cagney Productions' next film, *Blood in the Sun*. Always willing to try something new, Jimmy trained with martial arts expert Ken Kuniyuki and a former policeman named Jack Halloran to do his own stunts in the film. After the failure of *Johnny Come Lately*, the brothers hoped that the spy thriller set in Japan would be more appealing to American audiences. However, while *Blood in the Sun* was popular with critics and even won an Academy Award for Best Art Direction, it was a box office failure. Compounding that failure, Cagney had spotted a photo of a young war hero named Audie Murphy and believed that Murphy had the looks and poise to make it in pictures, so he invited him to Hollywood for a screen test. Unfortunately, Cagney didn't recognize the acting talent of the future actor and thus sold his contract to another company shortly after.

While trying to line up the rights for Cagney Productions' third movie, Cagney starred in *13 Rue Madeleine*, a spy picture that paid him $300,000. The film was a success, and Cagney used the money he made to produce *The Time of Your Life*, an adaptation of the Broadway play by the same name that appealed to critics but not to audiences. The problem was not Cagney's acting ability but the unwillingness of the public to accept him in the role of Joseph T., a quiet, philosophical people watcher.

During the years following World War II, Cagney became increasingly active in local and national political circles, an interest that had been sparked in the 1930s when he opposed the "Merriam Tax," a form of "under the table" bribes given by studios to the campaign of Frank Merriam, California's candidate for governor. Each actor was expected to donate a day's pay to Merriam's campaign, but out of principle, Cagney not only refused to make the required contribution, he also threatened to donate a week's salary to Merriam's opponent.

At first, Cagney considered himself to be a political liberal, and he supported Franklin Roosevelt's election and policies. He was also involved in what he later described as a "liberal group...with a leftist slant". However, when another member, future president Ronald Reagan, warned him about the direction the group was taking, he and Reagan resigned. Furthermore, his one-time involvement in the Anti-Nazi League caused him problems as the Red Scare and Cold War became everyday facts of life in post-war America, but thankfully he was ultimately cleared by the notorious House Un-American Activities Committee.

Furthermore, while serving as the president of the Screen Actors Guild in 1942 and 1943, Cagney led the Guild's opposition to the Mafia. There had been rumors for years about a group affectionately dubbed the "Irish Mafia" that Cagney himself was allegedly a member of, consisting of a group of Irish-American actors that like to get together for dinner and drinks, but by the early 1940s, Cagney found himself up against the real thing, an organized crime family that wanted to get their cut of the Hollywood action. Unlike many of his fellow actors, Cagney has seen guys like these before, and even after his wife got a call telling her that she was now a widow, he was unperturbed. When they stepped up their threats by hiring a hit man, Cagney contacted his friend George Raft, who apparently had his own underworld ties. He "made a call", and the hit was called off.

While Cagney had liked Roosevelt, he was not as fond of Harry Truman, so in 1948 he voted for a Republican candidate (Thomas E. Dewey) for the first time in his life. The next two decades saw him become firmly entrenched as a conservative, and Cagney explained this transition in his autobiography: "I believe in my bones that my going from the liberal stance to the conservative was a totally natural reaction once I began to see undisciplined elements in our country stimulating a breakdown of our system. From what I've seen of the liberal attitudes toward the young and the permissive attitude in the schools and everybody pulling every which way from center, I consider these all inimical to the health of our nation. Those functionless creatures, the hippies, for example, just didn't appear out of a vacuum."

Chapter 6: Mr. Cagney Meets Mr. Roberts

"Made it ma! Top of the world!" – Cagney's character in *White Heat*

The string of failed pictures left Cagney's own production company in deep debt, so Cagney made a deal to return to Warner Bros. with his company coming in as part of the deal, and the first picture made under the new agreement was *White Heat* in 1949. Unlike his previous characters, many of whom seemed to have a good reason for killing, Cagney's character (Cody Jarrett) was the mentally ill son of a man who had died in an insane asylum. He also had serious mother issues, even sitting in his elderly mother's lap at times. Not surprisingly, he dies a dramatic death at the end, killed in a massive explosion after gunning down some of his own men and shouting one of the most famous final quotes in a movie, "Made it ma! Top of the world!".

Cagney in *White Heat*

The studio called the movie the story of a "homicidal paranoiac with a mother fixation", and Cagney didn't disappoint. His performance in *White Heat* is considered one of his best, and in one of the most famous scenes, he did an impromptu take in the scene where Jarrett learns of the death of his mother that fellow actors didn't know was coming. His portrayal was so realistic and terrifying that it frightened some of his fellow cast members. The critics and the public both loved *White Heat*, but Cagney wasn't as happy with it. In spite of being America's "Yankee Doodle Dandy," he was still struggling against his gangster archetype, and by this time he was also the father of young children. As such, he told one reporter, "It's what the people want me to do. Someday, though, I'd like to make another movie that kids could go and see."

Cagney and Virginia Mayo in *White Heat*

In light of these feelings, it's no surprise that he jumped at the chance to star in another musical, this time opposite one of his favorite leading ladies, Doris Day. The musical was called *The West Point Story*, and Cagney said of it in his autobiography, "There was some critical thinking and hollering about the key plot line: the assignment of a Broadway musical director to actually live the life of a West Point cadet for some weeks. Such a thing just couldn't happen, some critics said. Only it did. Both Westbrook Pedlar and George M. Cohan did just that at various times."

However, Cagney's next film, *Kiss Tomorrow Goodbye*, brought him back to portraying a gangster, mostly because Cagney Productions, which had been purchased by Warner Bros., was deeply in debt. Having been raised to always pay his own bills, Cagney would not declare bankruptcy, and he insisted on making and marketing *Kiss Tomorrow Goodbye* to make money. Though the critics did not care for it, the public did, and they bought enough tickets to pay off Cagney's creditors. The company made just one more film, *A Lion is in the Streets*, and then shut down.

Cagney particularly enjoyed his next role as Martin "Moe the Gimp" Snyder in the 1955 movie *Love Me or Leave Me*, which he called "that extremely rare thing, the perfect script." Doris Day played his wife, Ruth Etting, in this biographical piece, and since Snyder was Jewish, it allowed Cagney to use the accent he had mastered when he was growing up on the Lower East Side. He also mastered Martin's limp to such an extent that Snyder himself asked Cagney how he did it. Cagney simply replied, "What I did was very simple. I just slapped my foot down as I turned it out while walking. That's all." Critics loved the film, and Cagney was nominated for another

Academy Award. He certainly would've won is the award was chosen by co-star Doris Day, who called Cagney "the most professional actor I've ever known. He was always 'real'. I simply forgot we were making a picture. His eyes would actually fill up when we were working on a tender scene. And you never needed drops to make your eyes shine when Jimmy was on the set."

Doris Day

Cagney in *Love Me Or Leave Me*

Next, Cagney worked with legendary director John Ford on *What Price Glory?*, but Cagney was not crazy about working with the famous director because Ford insisted the film be shot as a regular picture rather than the musical Cagney had signed on to make. Cagney would later refer to Ford having a "slightly sadistic sense of humor," which included allowing him and another actor to be injured in a motorcycle collision on set. The two nearly came to blows, as Cagney later recounted, "I would have kicked his brains out. He was so goddamned mean to everybody. He was truly a nasty old man." On another occasion, as Ford yelled at him, Cagney got back in his face, "When I started this picture, you said that we would tangle asses before this was over. I'm ready now – are you?" After that, Ford finally backed down.

John Ford

Given his dislike of Ford, it is somewhat surprising that Cagney agreed to make his next picture, *Mister Roberts*, with him, but Cagney wanted to work with his friend Spencer Tracy, who was supposed to play opposite him in the film. It was only after he had agreed to make the movie that Tracy was replaced by Henry Fonda, but he enjoyed working with Jack Lemmon, whom he described as "a nice young fella". In his autobiography, Cagney recalled the following story:

"I realized that upcoming was a scene with Jack, as Ensign Pulver, that I'd found so funny in the reading that I realized it would be marvelously so in the playing. The difficulty was that it was so funny I had serious doubts about my ability to play it with a straight face. I talked it over with Jack. I said, 'We've got some work ahead of us. You and I'll have to get together and rehearse that scene again and again and again until I don't think it's funny anymore.' He agreed because he had the same feeling about the scene. So we got together and did it and did it and did it. But every time I came to the payoff line in the scene, 'Fourteen months, sir,' I just couldn't keep a straight face. Finally, with enough rehearsal we thought we had it licked. We came to filming time.

"....This is one hell of a funny little scene: the commanding officer of a naval vessel finally meeting an ensign who had been ducking him during their voyage for well over a year. I used to collapse every time Jack said 'Fourteen months, sir,' but when we filmed it, I was able to hang on just barely. What you see in the film is the top of Mount Everest for us after our rigorous rehearsals. It still kills me every time I think about it."

Cagney wasn't the only one who thought the scene (and the entire film) was hilarious. The movie received three Oscar nominations, including one for Best Supporting Actor for that "nice young fella," Lemmon.

Chapter 7: The Gangster Goes Straight

"The last curtain call is usually the best. When it's time to go, you should go." – James Cagney

Following the completion of *Mister Roberts*, Cagney bought a new 120 acre farm in Dutchess County, New York. He named it Verney farm and poured tremendous effort into making it a working business, and over time, he bought more of the surrounding property, growing the farm to 750 acres. His agricultural efforts earned him an honorary degree from Rollins College in Florida, but rather than just accept the award, he insisted on submitting a paper on soil conservation to justify receiving his degree.

One feature that all Cagney's farms had in common were their horses. When Cagney was born in 1899, horses were still the primary mode of transportation in America, and as a city boy, his family obviously owned no horses, but he always jumped at the chance to get to sit on the back of the nag that pulled the milk truck. As an adult, he enjoyed buying, breeding, raising, training, and talking about horses, and Giant Morgans, of the big feet, were his favorite breed.

By this time, Cagney was 56 years old but still going strong both physically and mentally. He made his next movie, *Tribute to a Bad Man*, for MGM. This film, one of his few Westerns, had actually been written for Spencer Tracy, but Tracy was unable to complete filming due to health issues, so Cagney took over. *Tribute to a Bad Man* did well at the box office, leading MGM to cast Cagney opposite Barbara Stanwyck in *These Wilder Years*. Cagney liked Stanwyck from their time together in vaudeville years earlier, and in an off-screen scene reminiscent of something out of the movies, the two old stars entertained their younger cast members with song-and-dance numbers from their youth.

Stanwyck

Unlike many of his counterparts, Cagney had no interest in appearing on television, but in 1956, he agreed to appear in *Soldiers From the War Returning* as a favor to his old friend, Robert Montgomery. Montgomery had his own series and needed a powerful performance to open the new season with, but when reporters cornered him with questions about future television appearances, Cagney made his position clear: "I do enough work in movies. This is a high-tension business. I have tremendous admiration for the people who go through this sort of thing every week, but it's not for me."

Having had success with several other biographical films, Cagney portrayed famous actor Lon Cheney in *Man of 1000 Faces*, and the critics ate his performance up, with one reporter calling it one of the best performances of his career. It also did well at the box office, earning a good return for its production company, Universal Studios.

During this era, it was common for well-seasoned actors to try their hand at directing, so in

1957, Cagney made his first and only venture behind the camera to shoot *Shortcut to Hell*. A remake of 1941's *This Gun For Hire*, the movie was based on the novel *A Gun For Sale* by Graham Greene. At first, Cagney believed that he would be a very effective director; when he made the movie for his friend, producer A.C. Lyles, he did it as a favor, and for his own enjoyment, refusing to be paid. This appealed to Lyles, since he had very little money invested in the picture, which Cagney was able to shoot in just 20 days. He would later say that 20 days as a director was plenty for him, remarking, "We shot it in twenty days, and that was long enough for me. I find directing a bore, I have no desire to tell other people their business".

Over the next few years, Cagney made a few other movies, and by this time, he had enough money and prestige to be picky about what he wanted to do, so these roles were some of his best. He was happy to play the role of the labor leader in *Never Steal Anything Small*. In this musical, one of the last he would ever make, he enjoyed a hilarious song and dance number with Cara Williams, who portrayed his girlfriend in the film.

After *Never Steal Anything Small*, Cagney took off and flew to Ireland, where he filmed *Shake Hands with the Devil* with the well-known English director Michael Anderson. Cagney's reasoning for playing an Irish Republican army officer was more personal than professional; for one thing, Cagney felt he could use some of his off time in Ireland to trace his family's roots. Also, he was increasingly concerned about the level of violence spreading in the country, and he was attracted to *Shake Hands with the Devil*'s anti-violence message. The critics loved the film, and many considered it one of the best performances of his final years of acting.

In 1960, Cagney brought his production company out of mothballs to produce *The Gallant Hours*, and critics loved his portrayal of Adm. William F "Bull" Halsey, who led the Guadalcanal campaign in the Pacific. Though the film was set during World War II, it was not a classic war movie but more of a psychological thriller, with the focus being on the impact of command on Halsey himself. Critics loved the movie, with one reporter saying, "It is Mr. Cagney's performance, controlled to the last detail, that gives life and strong, heroic stature to the principal figure in the film. There is no braggadocio in it, no straining for bold or sharp effects. It is one of the quietest, most reflective, subtlest jobs that Mr. Cagney has ever done."

Cagney's final career film prior to retirement was the comedy *One, Two, Three*. Director Billie Wilder insisted that he was the only one to play an ambitious, overworked Coca-Cola executive trying to establish a presence in West Berlin. While the film itself was funny, Cagney's experience in making it was nothing to laugh about. He was the consummate professional and accustomed to working with tight scripts and well-rehearsed actors, so when one scene took 50 takes to get right, he was at his wit's end. He also complained about one of his co-stars, "I never had the slightest difficulty with a fellow actor. Not until *One, Two, Three*. In that picture, Horst Buchholz tried all sorts of scene-stealing didoes. I came close to knocking him on his ass." For the first time in his long career, he actually considered walking out on the movie, but he stuck it out and completed the film. During his time on set, he also made a visit to the Dachau concentration camp on one of his days off, which made a lasting impact on his life.

Cagney retired after returning to America, and unlike many men who have enjoyed fame and success, Cagney relished retirement. He spent most of his time on his farms, with occasional trips to both coasts to go sailing. Though he often struggled with seasickness, Cagney was an avid sailor, and he kept seaworthy craft on both the West and East Coast so he could sail whenever he got the chance.

Cagney also took up painting during his retirement, and to improve, he took instructions from the famous Sergei Bongart, who later asserted Cagney was so talented he could have been a professional artist had he started younger. He even proudly displayed two of Cagney's works in his own home, but Cagney always admitted he was nothing more than an amateur and refused to sell any of his work. The only exception was one painting, which he sold to Johnny Carson for charity.

When not painting, sailing or farming, Jimmy and Billie Cagney spent time in New York, where they enjoyed hosting parties at a little place called the Silver Horn restaurant. Over time, they became close friends with the owner, Marge Zimmerman, and later, when Cagney's health began to fail because of diabetes, Zimmerman became a valued friend and caretaker for the couple. She took it upon herself to refine recipes and cook dishes that helped Cagney manage both his diabetes and his cholesterol, which was also out of control. Under her careful care, Cagney lost weight and became healthier than he had been in years.

In 1974, Cagney made a rare public appearance to accept an American Film Institute Lifetime Achievement Award. Charlton Heston hosted the event, Frank Sinatra introduced Cagney, and so many stars showed up for the ceremony that one reporter quipped that if a bomb should go off in the building, the movie industry in America would be over. For his part, Cagney had fun at the ceremony, teasing impressionist Frank Gorshin by saying, "Oh, Frankie, just in passing, I never said 'MMMMmmmm, you dirty rat!' What I actually did say was 'Judy, Judy, Judy!'". Cagney's joke was a reference to another popular misquote of him, that one being attributed to Cary Grant.

A few years later, in 1977, Cagney had a small stroke, and though he recovered, he was no longer able to enjoy many of the physical sports that he had in the past, including dancing, which he had done to keep fit, and horseback riding, which he enjoyed for the thrill. He also became depressed and gave up painting. Zimmerman and Billie both devoted all their efforts to caring for and encouraging him, with the former becoming their full-time companion, and together, the two women persuaded Cagney to come out of retirement for one role, the small but critical part of New York Police Commissioner Rhinelander Waldo in the film version of the novel *Ragtime*.

Ironically, this American classic was shot in London, and since he never liked flying, Cagney traveled to England on a cruise, the *QEII*. When he arrived at Southampton, the cruise line officials were shocked to find their honored guest and most important passenger mauled by hundreds of fans. While Cagney's performance in *Ragtime* was strong, his co-stars had some problems; seasoned but younger actors missed their cues and forgot their lines in the face of the legend. One of them, Howard E. Rollins, Jr., recalled, "I was frightened to meet Mr. Cagney. I asked him how to die in front of the camera. He said 'Just die!' It worked. Who would know more about dying than him?" Rollins' reference to Cagney's many death scenes as a gangster aside, Cagney enjoyed playing the part, and in spite of increasing back pain, he remained on set after he was done filming to help the younger actors learn their lines.

In spite of his failing health, Cagney remained a star right up until the end of his life. When he and Pat O'Brien showed up at the Queen Mother's birthday performance at the London Palladium, the monarch rose to her feet at their entrance, the only time she stood up during the entire performance. A few years later, Cagney, now wheelchair-bound, appeared on television in *Terrible Joe Moran*, the story of an aging retired boxer. In flashback scenes, the director was able to make use of some of Cagney's early boxing footage in 1932's *Winner Take All*.

Terrible Joe Moran would be his final appearance, because Cagney died two years later on Easter Sunday morning of 1986 at his Dutchess County farm. His funeral mass was held at St. Frances de Sales Roman Catholic Church, with sitting president and old friend Ronald Reagan delivering the eulogy. Afterward, his body was buried at Hawthorne, New York's Cemetery of the Gate of Heaven.

Fittingly, Cagney wrote his own eulogy via the end of his autobiography, and as was his habit, he was more interested in talking about others than himself; in this case, he told his fans, "Thanks, too, for buying the ticket that gave me this lovely and deeply loved farm whence these words come. And, above all, the very numbers of those tickets prompt me to say: grateful thanks for giving a song and dance man across the years all those heartwarming encores."

Bibliography

Bergman, Andrew. James Cagney : The Pictorial Treasury of Film Stars (1974)

Cagney, James. Cagney by Cagney (2010)

Clinch, Minty. James Cagney (1982)

Federal Bureau of Investigations. James Cagney - The FBI Files (2012)

McCabe, John. Cagney (2013)

Schickel, Richard. James Cagney, A Life In Film (Movie Greats) (2012)

James Cagney: Paperback Book (Applause Legends) (2000)

Warren, Doug. James Cagney: The Authorized Biography (1983)

Edward G. Robinson

Chapter 1: Social Injustice and American Opportunity

It is safe to say that Edward G. Robinson's childhood began in a very different place from where it ended. Robinson was not born in the United States, and it was not until his early adolescence that his family opted to undergo a dramatic culture change and immigrate to America. He was born in Bucharest, Romania on December 12, 1893. Robinson's parents were Morris Goldenberg and Sarah Guttman; the name given to Edward at birth was Emanuel Goldenberg—he would later change his name in an attempt to make it more Anglican (which was seen as more marketable for aspiring actors.)

The Goldenberg's were Jewish, and Yiddish was spoken around the house (the children also learned Hebrew, Russian, and German). Their ties to the homeland reached deep, and it is believed that they had lived in Romania (or Rumania, as it is known in the native land) for 200 years, well before the Treaty of Berlin in 1878. The Treaty had made life difficult for Jews, denying them equal rights. Indeed, they were unable to attend universities, and many of the more desirable jobs were unavailable.

Thus, Robinson was born into a social climate that was hostile, at best, toward Jews. The family was fortunate, however, that his father, Morris, remained employed as a builder and tinsmith. They were working class but never wanting for food and lived in housing that was at least a rung above the ghetto in the social ladder. This was a period in which roughly 40 percent of Jews were unemployed due to restrictions against their opportunities, yet Morris maintained his jobs. The family was incredibly close, and Edward had four older brothers: Jack, Zach, Oscar, and Willie. After giving birth to Edward, Morris and Sarah had a sixth son, Max. Living quarters were tight, and all the more so due to the fact that Edward's grandmother lived with the family as well. The home was two stories, but the property had been assigned to them, and the setting was relatively sparse (Gansberg). What the setting lacked in amenities it made up for in community; Edward's family was part of a vibrant Jewish culture. Venturing outside of the neighborhood posed a great challenge—one that would ultimately prove responsible for the family's relocation to America. One day, Edward's brother, Jack, was attacked after leaving the neighborhood. A gang of anti-Semitic Romanians cracked his skull. He was not treated by a doctor, yet his skull appeared to heal on its own. However, the effects of the incident would linger, and Edward's brother remained mentally challenged for the rest of his life.

Morris and Sarah had been able to cope with the prejudice inflicted upon them for decades, but the critical condition that their son was placed in led them to reevaluate whether it was feasible to remain in Europe. Edward's family was hardly alone in this regard, and by the turn of the century, Jews were migrating en masse to the United States. Morris and Sarah opted to make the move to America early in the 20th century. They did not leave as a group; Zach was the first to arrive. He was succeeded by Jack and Oscar, after which Edward arrived with his parents. They moved to the Lower East Side of Manhattan, which at the time was a popular region of the city for immigrant families (Ross).

When Edward's family arrived in America, they were away from the unsafe conditions that had made it prudent for them to leave, but life in America was hardly comfortable (at least at first), as they spoke no English. For Edward, who was 10 years of age and just entering his adolescence, the culture change could not have been more difficult. To begin with, upon his arrival, he spoke not one word of English. He was enrolled at PS 137, but even though he was naturally blessed with great intelligence, the language barrier at first made it difficult for him to demonstrate his intellectual capabilities. Making matters worse, he was a terrible athlete, a quality that only made him more unpopular with his peers. Over time, he would rise to the top of the class but only after a difficult transitional period.

For his part, Morris fully bought into the American ideal of upward mobility, and he would impress upon his son the importance of climbing up the social ladder. Morris gave Edward the seemingly bizarre (or at least unpractical) advice to live beyond his means, with the rationale that this would force him to work hard enough to make ends meet—regardless of how difficult this might seem at a given point in time. In short time, Morris was able to rise above the relatively low social standing he had held in Romania. He opened a candy store, and Edward saw firsthand that it would be possible for him to find lucrative opportunities in America. Where Morris's economic advancement had operated in the realm of entrepreneurship, Edward held different ambitions, intending to become a criminal lawyer. It is worth noting, though, that this dream was not only due to the generous income earned by lawyers but also due to the fact that he wanted a profession "with the object of defending those who lacked the power or the money or the sense to defend themselves" (Gansberg). Robinson may have made a name for himself in Hollywood playing villainous gangster anti-heroes, but one can see from this example that his off-screen persona was indeed deeply altruistic.

As Edward gained fluency with the English language, his grades improved dramatically. His academic success led to his gaining admission to Townsend Harris High School at age 12, a more exclusive institution located further uptown. By this point, Morris was earning a decent living and was able to afford the relocation. At around the time that he began his studies at Townsend, Edward briefly toyed with wanting to be a rabbi when he grew up; at Morris's nudging, however, this dream ran its course, and he returned to his earlier desire to become a lawyer. His early teenage years also saw Edward become politically active for the first time, and he became enamored with William Randolph Hearst and journalism. Edward was, in short, a Renaissance man, someone who possessed a diverse range of interests and intellectual competencies.

While Edward displayed a talent for academics, one will notice that his interest in acting lay undeveloped through this early teenage years. Morris had been a fan of the theater and cinema and had taken Edward to weekend matinee showings. However, acting and the arts represented more of a diversion than a possible avenue for future employment. It would be several years before he saw acting as a viable career path. After graduating from Townsend Harris High School, he opted not to go into acting but decided, instead, to attend the City College of New York. This was a practical school to attend, as it meant that he would not need to relocate outside of the city. After enrolling, though, he became increasingly interested in acting, leading him to apply to the Sargent School, which would later become known as the American Academy of the Dramatic Arts. Upon applying, he suspected that he would never get in (he felt that his audition had not gone particularly well), yet he was admitted with a full scholarship (Gansberg). Robinson enrolled immediately, before concluding his studies at the City College of New York. He may have lacked a college degree, but the seeds were finally planted for a career in acting.

Chapter 2: Acting Education and Early Career

"In those days I would go for an interview and find myself competing with this other chap who would always be younger and taller, and much handsomer than I." – Edward G. Robinson

As his childhood makes clear, the acting career of Edward G. Robinson was hardly something that someone could have foreseen years in advance. To begin with, he had never been a star actor during his youth. Moreover, where many actors are autodidacts, more at home on the stage than in the organized arena of the classroom, Robinson actually displayed strong academic acumen. Plus, Robinson simply was not a glamorous young man. Short, round, and without looks that one would have described as conventionally attractive, Edward did not look like someone that one would identify as an actor. To be sure, his decision to matriculate in acting school was due to a love for the dramatic arts, not because he had the glamorous looks to earn easy money.

Edward's time at the Sargent School produced immediate changes, not only to his acting but also to his identity. One of the first changes that Sargent implemented was to have Edward Anglicize his first and last names. Up until this point, Robinson had been known as Emanuel Goldenberg, which Sargent believed was too Jewish. There was, of course, a rich lineage of Jewish vaudeville stars, but for Robinson to achieve the kind of broader cultural success that he would later acquire, it was felt that he would need a more gentile first and last name. Edward decided on his new names himself, and he was able to pass for a Gentile man—this is corroborated by the fact that Robinson would later play characters of various ethnicities. Changing his name was an important early step in the construction of his acting persona, although it must also be noted that the name change reflects the way in which arriving in America had not cleansed Robinson of being the victim of anti-Jewish prejudices.

A benefit to being a student at the Sargent School was that Robinson was able to complete his coursework while simultaneously receiving actual acting experience. He was able to compensate somewhat for his height deficit through wearing lifts in his shoes. In fact, it was while he was enrolled in acting school that he made his stage debut, in a production of Henrik Ibsen's famous *The Pillars of Society* (1877). Then, in 1913, Edward achieved what was at this stage of his career a breakthrough, staging his own production. The play, titled *The Bells of Conscience*, was based on a short story by Henry James. This play succeeded to a greater degree than he could have hoped, and Loew's gave him the opportunity to perform at the famous Plaza Theater on Lexington Avenue in New York City. The production was met with general acclaim, although it did not lead to other opportunities.

Edward completed his acting studies in 1913 at 20 years of age. Even though he had already staged his own Broadway production, Robinson found it difficult to make further headway. As one might suspect, this was due in large part to his lack of a conventionally handsome frame— Robinson simply did not embody the stereotypical appearance of the male actor. Fortunately, a longtime friend of his, Pepe Schildkraut, was the son of Rudolph Schildkraut, a notable figure in the Yiddish theater. Rudolph was able to arrange for Edward to get hired for a small role in a production of *Number 37* (1913). Interestingly, his name was listed on the program as Edward Golden.

Even though *Number 37* occupies little more than a footnote in the career of Edward G. Robinson, his performance is worth noting, since Robinson played a district attorney in his 50s, despite being just 20 years old at the time. *Number 37* featured a predominantly Jewish cast, and in the Yiddish theater, it was not uncommon for young actors to play characters who were much older. There is also a dose of irony to the fact that Robinson successfully portrayed a man in his 50s, since Robinson's own acting career would begin to suffer by the time he reached his late 50s.

Rudolph Schildkraut

Once *Number 37* had run its course, Robinson again found himself without gainful employment, a difficult predicament for a man whose natural intelligence would surely have led to a successful job as a lawyer or engineer. With no attractive alternative, he accepted a job with the S.M. Steinbach Stock Company, which hired him as an apprentice. This entailed a range of responsibilities, including pulling curtains and running basic errands for the staff. His pay was $25 per week, which was a paltry sum even for the standards of the time period. The job did take him outside of New York City for the first time in more than a decade, though, and the company performed in Binghamton, New York. There was also, in fact, greater motivation for joining the company than serving as a stagehand. Robinson suspected that he might gain the opportunity to appear in several productions, and he was right. His most significant performance was as Sato in a 1914 production of Eugene Walter's *Paid in Full* (1908). This proved to be a major event for Robinson's career, as it led him to get cast in *Under Fire* (1915).

In the career of an actor, several breakthroughs often are necessary before one solidifies a place for himself in the industry. If *Bells of Conscience* had constituted his first such achievement, *Under Fire* was the second. His salary for the production began at $60 per week but was raised to $80 following the production's initial success. The play opened in April of 1915 and received excellent reviews. It reached Broadway, and Robinson would no longer have to suffer to find acting opportunities. For the first time, he also gained financial independence, allowing him to find a place to live in New York City that was outside the crowded confines of his parents' home. Indeed, as Alan Gansberg explains, Robinson became something of a dandy, a "man about town": "With his newfound success, Robinson…bought an entirely new wardrobe, all first class, remembering what Morris Goldenberg [his father] had always told him about living beyond his means so he'd work harder. He strutted down Broadway carrying a cane, wearing spats: a dandy, a man of distinction, a man girls wanted to date. And date he did, always taking a taxi and doing it right." Robinson was finally able to not only act well but also to look the part of the well-to-do young actor. He maintained a vibrant social life, yet as Gansberg reveals, Edward was conscious of always behaving in good taste. He dated many women, but it would be a number of years before he actually got married.

The productions that Robinson appeared in following *Under Fire* were of relatively minor acclaim, although he was never truly lacking work. He was cast in *Under Sentence* (1916), a play written by Mergrue and Irvin S. Cobb. This was followed by *The Pawn*, which opened in September of 1917. It lasted just two weeks, though, and Robinson moved on to a production of *Drafted* (1917), but it too flopped immediately after opening. More successful was a production of *The Deluge*, which opened in November of 1917. Robinson had been hired for the production by well-decorated producer Arthur Hopkins, but it was not the landmark production he had hoped it would become.

Considering that Robinson was in his mid-20s when the United States entered World War I, it would be fair to expect that he would enlist in the conflict. In fact, Robinson enlisted in the

Navy, where he was sent as a sailor to Pelham Bay in the Bronx. This was obviously a far cry from the armed combat that was taking place overseas, and Robinson's duties consisted of menial activities like peeling potatoes and other such tasks (Gansberg).

   After the Armistice was signed, he was hired by the Garrick Players in Washington, D.C. His time with the company lasted a couple of months, after which he returned to New York City. His career was slowed down by the fact that times were changing in the theater industry. In 1919, a major actors strike took place, and Robinson (who, since the days when he had wanted to be a lawyer, had been politically-conscious) joined in the effort. Before the end of 1919, he was back to working and was cast in a production of *Dark Horses* (1919). The following year, he and his good friend Sam Jaffe then acted together in *Samson and Delilah*. Headlining the production was not Robinson or Jaffe but rather, the legendary Yiddish actor Jacob Ben-Ami. A personality clash unfolded on the set, as Robinson and Jaffe found it impossible to work with their more famous co-star, who exuded a pompous air (Gansberg). Still, the play earned Robinson greater exposure, and it was productive in furthering his career.

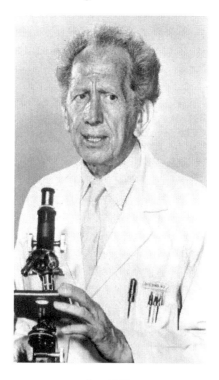

Sam Jaffe

   By the early 1920s, the film industry had already largely usurped theater as the most popular form of entertainment in mass culture, but even though Robinson had always enjoyed movies (dating back to his weekend excursions with his father), it was difficult for him to gain entry into the industry. It would be several years before the motion picture industry converted to sound, and actors had to rely exclusively on their appearance in order to gain acting opportunities during this time. For someone like Robinson, whose success in the theater had been largely due to his verbal delivery, it was difficult for him to break into cinema.

However, it was through the intervention of Arthur Hopkins that he was able to find a fairly significant role in the 1923 movie *The Bright Shawl*. Technically, Robinson had made his film debut seven years earlier in an extremely minor (and uncredited) role in a small picture. *The Bright Shawl*, on the other hand, was a big-budget picture with significant star power. The movie starred Dorothy Gish, Mary Astor, and Richard Barthelmess. Amidst such a famous cast, Robinson's own role is not especially major, but the historical drama (set in Cuba during the unsuccessful revolution of 1850) earned good reviews.

Dorothy Gish

During the middle of the decade, Robinson's acting remained fixed within the domain of theater, and he continued to maintain a rather lively social life. As a well-to-do Broadway actor, he held a prominent position among the Manhattan socialites, and it was in this context that he met Gladys Lloyd, his future wife. Lloyd was a theater actress, although she would also venture into cinema during the early 1930s and appearing in some of Robinson's own pictures. While

Robinson had been raised in an immigrant family, Lloyd came from a privileged family background as the daughter of Clement Cassell, a well-known sculptor and architect. Despite the fact that Lloyd was younger than Edward, she had already been married once to Ralph L. Vestervelt. Robinson and Lloyd never appeared to possess strong chemistry with one another, but their relationship progressed swiftly, and they were married in 1927.

Robinson was already well into his 30s, and while he was undeniably a social person, romance and marriage were not the priorities for him that they were for most men during the 1920s. Six years after their marriage, Gladys would give birth to a son, Edward G. Robinson, Jr. Gladys also had a daughter from her first marriage who was raised by her and Edward. Edward and his wife were not exactly a romantic couple, but they were one of the most visible celebrity couples in New York City (and later in Hollywood), frequently hosting extravagant parties. Robinson proved to be an adept host, and a stark contrast emerged between the irascible characters he would become famous for onscreen and the graceful presence he maintained in his social life.

Robinson and Gladys Lloyd

1927 was a major year in Robinson's life not just for his marriage but also because he was cast in a theatrical role that would have implications on his film career. That year, he was cast in the leading role in *The Racket*, playing a combustible gangster. The part marked a sizable change from the more verbal characters he had played in the past; in this play, Edward's role was characterized by the anger of his character rather than his verbal wit. The play performed well on Broadway, and Robinson demonstrated that he could convincingly play the role of the angry criminal, a talent that would lead to him getting cast in major Hollywood films shortly thereafter.

The other substantial development that facilitated Edward's entry into the film industry was the development of synchronized sound cinema. In 1927, the outstanding success of *The Jazz Singer* convinced Hollywood that sound would be a lucrative initiative. In hindsight, it is easy to overlook just how expansive the changes to the industry were, and it was no easy decision for American film producers to shift to sound; not only did production circumstances need to be altered to accommodate sound, theaters had to be wired for sound, a costly proposition that put many less-successful theaters out of business. In addition, many actors and actresses had made names for themselves on the basis of their skills as silent actors, and as *Singin' in the Rain* (1952) memorably depicts, it was challenging for those with untrained voices to suddenly make their voices heard to everyone.

However, as someone who had succeeded in theater largely due to his vocal talents, Edward G. Robinson was well-poised for success in sound film, even as it's fair to wonder whether his movie career would have ever gained traction in a silent era.

J. Carrol Naish and Robinson in *Two Seconds* (1932)

"I had the advantage of reading the book, and when the script was first submitted to me, it was just another gangster story - the east side taking over the west side and all that." – Edward G. Robinson

When Robinson returned to movies in 1928, five years had elapsed since his performance in *The Bright Shawl*. It was under the encouragement of famed producer Walter Wanger that he pursued film acting once again, and his next movie, *The Hole in the Wall* (1929), followed closely in the footsteps of *The Racket*. The film was a large-budget picture, with Claudette Colbert starring alongside Robinson. In fact, it is Colbert who occupies the main role as a woman who attempts to exact vengeance against the woman who sent her to prison. As one would expect, Robinson plays a gangster, and the movie is one of the first examples of the gangster genre that, along with the musical, would dominate Hollywood during the following decade. The movie also involves an unlikely romance between Colbert—who would become known for family melodramas—and Robinson. After he became famous, Robinson would disown the picture, but while it is not an exemplary film in its genre, the surprising chemistry between Robinson and his co-star makes the movie worth viewing.

Wanger

Colbert

The Hole in the Wall inaugurated a remarkably prolific run for Edward G. Robinson that saw him act in roughly 100 movies over the next 30 years. In 1930, he starred in six movies, and while some of them are either shorts or have lost circulation over time, these early films gave him the opportunity to work with some decorated figures in American film. Two of the pictures made in 1930, for example, were made under the supervision of decorated producer Carl Laemmle, a German expatriate. One of the two Laemmle films, *Outside the Law*, was directed by Tod Browning, who is now a legendary cult figure for his later horror movies. *Outside the Law* was a remake of a film of the same name that had starred Lon Chaney, and the 1930 version cast Robinson in the role of Cobra Collins, a gangster boss who attempts to circumvent a heist undertaken by a rival gang. His performance exudes the gravitas of Robinson's later gangster characters, and he comes across as the very embodiment of the angry, jaded, and vengeful gangster.

The 1930 movies in which Robinson appeared paled in comparison to his first movie from the next year, the legendary *Little Caesar*. It goes without saying that *Little Caesar* established Robinson's standing in Hollywood, and it stands alongside *Public Enemy* (1931) and *Scarface* (1932) among the premier examples of the genre. Since it was released immediately before these other two films, *Little Caesar* is perhaps the most significant of the three, laying the groundwork for the genre (Shadoian). Where Robinson had been relegated to the role of co-star in *The Hole in the Wall*, in *Little Caesar* it is he—in the role of gangster Caesar Enrico "Rico" Bandello— who undeniably remains the main attraction. This was an accomplishment, seeing as *Little*

Caesar boasted a strong supporting cast that included Douglas Fairbanks, Jr. and Glenda Farrell.

   In the movie, Rico and his good friend Joe (Fairbanks) play small-town men who arrive in Chicago with the intention of making it rich. After arriving, they move in separate directions; Joe pursues a career as a dancer, while Rico joins a gang and rises through the ranks of organized crime. He attempts to coerce Joe into joining him in a life of crime, but his friend is unable to accept life as a criminal. Rico realizes that his friend is dangerous, yet he cannot bring himself to kill him. This ultimately leads to his downfall, as Joe provides secrets to the authorities, who eventually use the information to kill Rico.

Robinson and Fairbanks in the trailer for *Little Caesar*

One of the reasons that *Little Caesar* and other representative films of the gangster genre are so effective is that the ambitions that Rico holds bear some resemblance to the myth of the American Dream. To be sure, the vast majority of Americans were uninterested in killing others or engaging in criminal activity, but Rico's ambition to arrive in the city and make his fortune was not far removed from the reasons why many others arrived in the urban landscape. At the same time, the failure of the gangster hero, whose death always occurs at the conclusion of the film, serves to mark the way in which the American Dream was not always attainable. Robert Warshow has elaborated on this theme, describing how such films chart a trajectory from optimism to defeat: "Even within the area of mass culture, there always exists a current of opposition [against the American Dream], seeking to express by whatever means are available to it that sense of desperation and inevitable failure which optimism itself helps to create…The gangster film is remarkable in that…From its beginning, it has been a consistent and astonishingly complete presentation of the modern sense of tragedy."

Referring to gangster films as tragedies may seem surprising since the criminal is invariably brought to justice in the end, but by referring to the gangster as a tragic figure, Warshow implicitly identifies how the gangster is a sympathetic villain, someone who behaves differently from the common American but shares the same basic desire for economic success and fame. As a bombastic anti-hero, Robinson is, in certain respects, a figure the viewer loves to hate, but the effectiveness of such films also rests in the underlying sense of failed ambition that runs across both Robinson's character and the viewer as well.

Robinson in the trailer for _Little Caesar_

Little Caesar was by far the most important gangster film to emerge from the American cinema up to that point in time, but this was due more to its subject matter (as well as Robinson's chilling performance) than to its formal qualities. Viewers accustomed to the stylized gangster pictures that have been released in more recent decades, such as Brian De Palma's remake of _Scarface_ (1983), may well find that _Little Caesar_ looks somewhat ordinary in terms of its special effects and visuals. This should not diminish an assessment of the film, however, and Jack Shadoian argues that the formal elements of the film are successful in squaring attention on Robinson's singular character: "Its stripped-to-the-bone minimalism gives _Little Caesar_ an obduracy of pace and style that is unique. It is a film that doesn't budge…The most restrained of gangster films, its Spartan efficiency is opportunely functional in defining and displaying its perversely animated central figure." Shadoian alludes to the extent to which Robinson absolutely dominates the film with his performance, a quality that only makes his character's death at the conclusion all the more dramatic.

Given that _Little Caesar_ was made in the early 1930s, during the late years of Prohibition, one might expect the film to stand either as a moralistic document affirming the virtues of dry America or a critique on the culture of organized crime that developed through Prohibition. In actuality, as Shadoian points out, _Little Caesar_ places little emphasis on critiquing society, instead emphasizing Robinson's character. In a similar vein, the film does not probe organized crime as a social phenomenon so much as it burrows into the mind of the particular gangster portrayed by Edward G. Robinson. Thus, to enjoy *Little Caesar* is to be captivated by the spectacle of Robinson as Rico the dangerous mobster.

Although it stands as a true classic of the 1930s, *Little Caesar* was not showered with Oscar nominations, as it was nominated only for Best Screenplay. More importantly for Robinson's career, the movie catapulted to the pinnacle of the gangster genre, and he would remain alongside James Cagney and a select few others in the elite ranks of the genre.

There is no doubt that *Little Caesar* was a difficult act to follow, but in terms of star power, Robinson's next picture, *Smart Money* (1931), proves every bit as impressive. The movie remains the only time in which Robinson and James Cagney appeared together in a picture. As with *Little Caesar*, *Smart Money* was distributed by Warner Brothers, which was easily the studio most invested in the genre. This was an era in which the genre system that characterized Hollywood was filtered predominantly through studios. MGM, for example, was recognized for its big-budget musicals and was also the wealthiest studio. In contrast, Paramount built its reputation on the back of light, sophisticated comedies, many of which were directed by prominent German expatriates. RKO, meanwhile, made somewhat more eclectic pictures on smaller budgets, and Warner Brothers was home to the gangster film, with Edward G. Robinson as perhaps the genre's defining star.

In *Smart Money*, it is Robinson who takes primacy over Cagney, although it is worth noting that the movie was filmed before the release of Cagney's iconic performance in *The Public Enemy*, a performance that made him roughly Robinson's equal.

The plot of *Smart Money* is not as over-the-top in its use of violence as *Little Caesar*. Robinson plays a crooked barber who partakes in high-stakes gambling, and Cagney serves as his accomplice. Unlike *Little Caesar*, Robinson's character does not die at the end (although he is arrested and sentenced to 10 years in prison), but Cagney's character is gunned down. Gone in *Smart Money* is the almost mythological nature of Robinson's character, and there is no doubt that the later film is not as memorable. It is best treated as a lighter effort that is enjoyable on its own merits but not a masterpiece. The chemistry between Robinson and Cagney is perhaps the highlight, and there is none of the competition between the two illustrious gangster antiheroes that viewers might have expected to encounter.

The movies that Robinson appeared in immediately following *Smart Money* continue in much the same vein, with the actor constantly starring in gangster roles. Many of these pictures are largely forgotten today, but they were popular in their historical context and contain intriguing aspects for 21st century viewers. In *Tiger Shark* (1932), for example, Robinson plays a fisherman with one hand, and the conflict centers on his relationship with his wife, who falls for the man whom Robinson lost his arm saving. As Peter Lehman identifies, the motif of the lost arm functions as a commentary on masculinity, with Robinson coded metaphorically as being impotent. Lehman argues that the "entire narrative trajectory is one of loss, and every aspect of his character is marked as inadequately masculine…Robinson's short, round body [functions] as a sign of a pervasive, failed masculinity." This astute reading of his character relates to the previous discussions of Robinson's unconventional appearance; he fell short (literally and metaphorically) of the masculine standard in Hollywood, and this opened the door for films that cast him in parts that were outside the norm for leading men in American cinema. In any event, *Tiger Shark* was directed by legendary director Howard Hawks, and while it is by no means one of the defining films of Hawks' career, it represents an interesting collaboration between one of the directors of the decade and one of the leading actors of the decade.

In the wake of *Tiger Shark*, Robinson continued his working relationship with Warner Brothers, although he did branch away from gangster films on occasion. An example of this can be seen in *The Man with Two Faces* (1934), which was directed by Archie Mayo and distributed by Warner Brothers. A suspenseful film, Edward was cast in the somewhat unlikely role of a stage actor, and Mary Astor stars as his sister, a famous actress who must escape her past, which includes a failed marriage to a criminal husband. Her ex-husband returns to haunt her, leading her to turn to her brother for assistance. He poisons the ex-husband but must exonerate himself from guilt. In an age when gangster films were still quite popular in Hollywood, it is refreshing to see a dramatically different effort from Robinson.

Mary Astor

One of the interesting developments in mid-1930s Hollywood is that at the same time that gangster films were devoured by the public, there also was a mild initiative to partake in the New Deal narrative of social uplift, thereby cleansing American entertainment of such characters. It is also important to note that by 1933, the Hays Code began getting more stringently enforced, which effectively abolished any overtly suggestive material in Hollywood films. In 1936, Robinson starred in *Bullets or Ballots*, which reworked his screen persona, but whereas many of his earlier films saw him play shady gangsters, in this film Robinson operates on the side of law enforcement, acting as a detective charged with breaking up a gang (with a very young Humphrey Bogart as one of its members).

Michael Szalay unpacks the peculiarities of Edward playing a detective, linking the casting decision to the politics of America at the time: "Doing its part for the New Deal in 1935, Warner Brothers transformed gangsters into government employees. In fact, the studio recast actors such as James Cagney and Edward G. Robinson (once "Public Enemy" and "Little Caesar," respectively) as federal and state agents ridding America of the gangsters they had originally immortalized." As Szalay suggests, it was believed that by cleansing Hollywood of its infamous gangster characters, Hollywood could promote the ethos of the New Deal, but the plan was not particularly successful, as Robinson returned to playing gangsters not long after *Bullets or Ballots* was released. An example of such a picture is *The Last Gangster* (1937). Robinson appears as Joe Krozac, a notorious gangster during Prohibition who marries Talya, a girl with no knowledge of his criminal past. It is only after Krozac is arrested for tax evasion that she becomes aware of his criminal status. While Joe is in prison, Talya begins a relationship with a newspaper reporter (played by James Stewart) profiling her husband, and the two eventually marry.

The Last Gangster is not only an engaging film on its own merits but also offers a fascinating glimpse into the dynamics of Hollywood at the time, specifically through the juxtaposition between Jimmy Stewart and Edward G. Robinson. It is noteworthy that it is Stewart who replaces Edward's character, and the film contrasts the socially-upstanding Stewart against the criminal Robinson. The dichotomy between the two men also extends to their physiques; notably taller and trimmer than Robinson, Stewart embodied a more conventionally handsome brand of masculinity than Robinson was able to achieve. Robinson's body was very much that of the gangster protagonist, and James Cagney, the other gangster hero, possessed a very similar frame. The short, round figures of Robinson and Cagney were effectively coded as illicit or deviant, while the lanky frame of Stewart and Henry Fonda epitomized the masculine standard. In this sense, it can be said that Edward G. Robinson's body offers a case study for the way in which the moral politics of Hollywood cinema were enacted through actors' bodies.

Jimmy Stewart

As the decade progressed, Robinson (and Warner Brothers) began to poke fun at and caricature his hard-boiled gangster image. In 1938, he starred in *A Slight Case of Murder*, a Warner Brothers parody of the gangster film in which Robinson plays Remy Marco, a bootlegger who loses money due to the fact that his beer tastes foul. *A Slight Case of Murder* showcased a more lighthearted dimension to Robinson, and the film was positively received. He would never come to be known for comedies, but the movie provided light entertainment and a kind of retrospective glance back at Robinson's earlier films.

If Robinson proved himself capable of poking fun at his earlier performances, his gangster image was nevertheless difficult to displace, and it wasn't as though he was attempting to shed this image. The same year as *A Slight Case of Murder*, he starred in *The Amazing Dr. Clitterhouse* (1938), one of the more bizarre gangster films of the decade. Robinson's character, the eponymous Dr. Clitterhouse, was a doctor who attempts to learn more about the pathology of criminals by becoming one himself. He is successful and convincing in his criminal activity, leading him to gain the favor of the mob boss (played by Humphrey Bogart). Eventually, he is arrested for his crimes but found not guilty on account of insanity.

In its exploration into the psychology of the criminal, the movie is more psychological than many of his earlier films, and in this respect, it anticipates the more existential film noir movies of the following decade. Another interesting change distancing *The Amazing Dr. Clitterhouse* from his previous mob films is that in this one, Robinson has shifted from mob boss (the position he occupied earlier in the decade) to an outsider who enters the criminal circle. Furthermore, given his legendary performances in *Casablanca* (1942) and other movies during the 1940s and 1950s, it is easy to forget Humphrey Bogart's affiliation with gangster movies, but during the 1930s, there was a way in which he served as a kind of successor to Robinson.

Of course, the late 1930s also are worthy of mention because they saw the arrival of World War II. While it would not be until early in the following decade that the United States was attacked at Pearl Harbor, Robinson became politically outspoken against Nazism and fascism. He had always been politically conscious, and he used his influence in Hollywood to galvanize support amongst his peers for the Allies. Even today, Hollywood is recognized as a left-leaning town, but in the late 1930s it was even more so, to the point that many actors were affiliated with the Communist Party. For his part, Robinson was not Communist, but in the closing months of 1938, he adopted an activist role, and he and 55 other members of the film industry organized the Committee of 56, which advocated for Congress to boycott any products made in Germany until the Nazis ended their atrocious crimes against Jews and other minorities and ethnicities (Ross). Steven Ross explains that "Robinson showed how a mobilized community of movie stars could use their celebrity to draw national attention to the most controversial issues of the day and help sway public opinion." Robinson is to be commended for acting from the heart, but as Ross notes, the majority of Americans actually opposed entering the war at the time: "Americans today like to talk nostalgically about World War Two as the 'Good War,' a war where 'good' and 'evil' were easy to identify. During the 1930s, however, the vast majority of Americans preferred to turn a blind eye to events in Europe." Eventually, of course, the United States entered the conflict, and Robinson remained one of the more politically active members of the Hollywood community.

Robinson's political interests and his Hollywood career intersected rather directly in 1939 when he starred in *Confessions of a Nazi Spy*. The movie was the first explicitly anti-Nazi movie produced by a major Hollywood studio (it was made by Warner Brothers), and the studio poured an enormous budget into the film, which cost $1.5 million to make. For a propaganda film, the movie is actually quite entertaining on its own merits; Robinson plays a doctor who captures a Nazi who has arrived in America to galvanize support for the Nazi cause. The movie made a terrific profit at the box office, and certain scenes were based on true events.

Chapter 4: Double Indemnity and Film Noir

"Things got so bad that when I went shopping for a house, some people would refuse to open the door if they saw it was me standing there. And drunks would always want to challenge me."
– Edward G. Robinson

The early 1940s saw Robinson act in a number of crime movies, and they generally veered closer to the gangster films of the 1930s than the film noir pictures that would emerge later in the decade. In 1940, he starred in *Brother Orchid*, playing crime leader Little John Sarto. He heads to Europe in an attempt to overcome his crude status but loses his money and finds himself forced to return to the United States and rejoin with his old gang. The movie concludes with him joining a monastery. One can see that the movie contains a somewhat moralistic theme, but the most compelling scenes involve Robinson with Humphrey Bogart, who plays the second in command in Robinson's gang. *Brother Orchid* is one among many gangster films that paired Robinson with Bogart; the reason behind the pairing was simple enough – Bogart and Robinson were both under contract with Warner Brothers. But the pairing also matched one of the premier actors of the 1930s (Robinson) with Bogart, who was himself arguably the most famous star of the 1940s.

Robinson and Bogart in *Brother Orchid*

In 1941, Robinson acted in the cinematic adaptation of Jack London's novel *The Sea Wolf*, playing the notorious sea captain. The movie was nominated for an Academy Award for Best Visual Effects. Later that same year, he was cast in *Manpower*, a remake of *Tiger Shark*, which had been released nearly one decade earlier. The primary difference between the two films is that where the former saw Edward play a disabled fisherman, in *Manpower* he plays an electric power lineman. The movie opened to generally positive reviews, although it is overshadowed by the movies he appeared in both in the decade prior and later in the 1940s.

Perhaps not surprisingly, Robinson ventured into the war film genre early during the 1940s. Given that the United States was deep in its involvement overseas during World War II, war films were extraordinarily popular during this time, and even though Robinson was turning 50, he received a prominent role in *Destroyer* (1943). In the movie, Robinson and Glenn Ford play sailors during World War II, and the decision to cast Robinson is somewhat surprising in light of the fact that he did not look particularly young for his age, but he and Glenn Ford display strong chemistry with one another, and *Destroyer* is an enjoyable, if overlooked, movie in Robinson's filmography.

Robinson and Lynn Bari in a publicity photo for *Tampico* (1944)

As interesting as *Destroyer* was, it was in 1944 that Robinson's career truly caught its second wind, as he began getting cast in film noirs and other pictures that reworked significant aspects of the gangster movies. In 1944, he starred in what was by far the most important noir of his career, *Double Indemnity*. The movie was directed by Billy Wilder, a widely lauded German expatriate who would remain one of the more praised Hollywood directors for the next couple of decades. Wilder was an ideal match for Robinson; the bleak gangster pictures Robinson had starred in during the 1930s were complemented nicely by Wilder's dark vision. George Stevens, Jr. elaborates on Wilder's personality: "Billy had a sardonic view of the world. His was a European outlook without the underlying optimism that colored so many of the films of his friends and colleagues in Hollywood. Walter Matthau once said that Billy saw the worst in the best of us and the best in the worst of us." Even from this brief description, one can see how Wilder would be a perfect match for Robinson, whose gangster films had always adopted a dark view of the American Dream.

In addition to Wilder, *Double Indemnity* benefitted from an all-star cast, including Barbara Stanwyck and Fred MacMurray. The film's budget actually was not as large as other movies Robinson had appeared in during the several years prior, but it was one of the most commercially successful movies of the time period. It was nominated for seven Academy Awards, including Best Picture, Best Director, and Best Cinematography, although it did not win any Oscars.

Robinson in *Double Indemnity*

Double Indemnity contains one of the most iconic of all noir plots. The plot involves a frustrated wife (played by Barbara Stanwyck) who wants to dispose of her husband. With this in mind, she seduces an insurance agent (Fred MacMurray) to kill her husband, realizing that she can collect a more robust insurance policy if he is killed through an automobile accident. MacMurray's character orchestrates the death so that the husband falls from a train, thus ostensibly allowing the wife to collect a "double indemnity" clause. However, MacMurray's colleague, Keyes (Robinson's character), is assigned to the case, and his meticulous sleuthing leads MacMurray to confess to the murder.

The plot of *Double Indemnity* contains many intricacies, although it is relatively simple when compared to other noir staples such as *The Maltese Falcon* (1941) or *The Big Sleep* (1946). There may be no noir film, however, that contains so many signature aspects of the genre. To begin with, the film contains voiceover narration provided by Fred MacMurray's character, such that he narrates the past from the vantage point of the future. This heightens the determinism of the plot, as the viewer can sense that MacMurray is guilty and no longer a free man. Indeed, the narrative essentially consists of a lengthy and intricate confession, suggesting that crime will not go unpunished, and that the criminal will be overridden with guilt and feel the need to confess. Billy Wilder was careful to stipulate, however, that the voiceover was more than a mere stylistic device, stating that "it is useful if there is a reason for it, if it is anchored in the story. I think in *Double Indemnity* it was very good because…There was a reason for telling the story that way" (Stevens, Jr. 326).

In addition to the voiceover, *Double Indemnity* contains Barbara Stanwyck's performance as one of the most famous femme fatales of all time. The viewer can sense that Stanwyck will only cause harm to MacMurray, and yet she is so alluring that MacMurray's decision to assist her in the act of crime is almost understandable and worthy of the viewer's identification. On the level of form and visual style, *Double Indemnity* also boasts a dramatic black-and-white aesthetic, replete with rich chiaroscuro. It is one of the most formally dramatic noir films, utilizing its dramatic lighting contrasts in order to embody the deeply existential pessimism of its theme.

Like many other noir films, *Double Indemnity* was not adapted from a culturally prestigious novel but from the hard-boiled crime fiction that had recently become popular in American literature. The film was based on the novel of the same name by James M. Cain, which had been published just one year prior to the film's release. It was important that noir adapted less culturally revered texts, as this gave the directors more leeway than if they were making a film based on a more canonized literary text, which would be viewed as more sacred and offer less room for modification on the part of the director. The hard-boiled texts were also somewhat racier than more decorated novels, which often made it difficult for noir to satisfy the draconian censorship regulations that were in place during the height of the Hays Code. To this end, *Double Indemnity* faced numerous challenges in its production process, and modifications were made, but as Naremore notes, "Even in its released form, *Double Indemnity* was an unorthodox film, challenging nearly a decade of Production Code resistance to James M. Cain's fiction."

Naremore expounds upon this by noting that, in particular, *Double Indemnity* was a target of censorship due to its almost attractive and sexy depiction of murder, its use of adultery, and the murder plot. These aspects may seem de rigeur for 21st century films, but in 1944, they presented a major obstacle.

Fred MacMurray, Barbara Stanwyck, and Robinson

As James Naremore and others have pointed out, film noir was a genre that was established retroactively by critics, not by the institution of Hollywood itself. This significantly distances film noir from the musical, the western, or the gangster film, and considering that noir was not actually manufactured as a cinematic genre, it is all the more remarkable that there was such a strong degree of coherence within the noir films. As a movement, noir lasted roughly from 1941 (with the release of *The Maltese Falcon*) through 1958 (with *Touch of Evil*). In addition, one of the important contributions made by James Naremore in his canonical study of noir is that the genre was not limited to America but encompassed British film as well. In short, it was possible for critics to look back and designate noir as a genre because a sizeable percentage of American and British films began addressing wartime (and postwar) existential themes of psychological unrest and masculine instability.

If film noir constituted the premier action genre of 1940s Hollywood and the gangster film fulfilled a similar function in the previous decade, it is only natural to compare the two. To begin with, film noir was more formally innovative and stylish, achieving what Gerd Gemunden explains as a deft blend between formal experimentation and realism: "Focusing on the depiction of an urban environment, *film noir* employs a mode of representation that while realist emphasizes abstraction and formal experiment, and it is informed by a critical or at least ambivalent stance about progress and modernity." Looking outside the level of form, in his lengthy study of Fritz Lang (with whom Robinson would work not long after *Double Indemnity*), Tom Gunning has posited that noir retains the dark sociological view intrinsic to gangster movies but that noir adds a strong dose of eroticism that had been dormant in the prior decade.

This certainly can be seen in comparing *Double Indemnity* with films such as *Little Caesar*. Although in many ways a helpless victim, Fred MacMurray was certainly closer to the standard of the Hollywood leading male than Edward G. Robinson. Robinson and Cagney were short and frequently cast as quick-tempered men who were, in many respects, almost infantile; MacMurray (and other noir leading men, including Robert Mitchum and Glenn Ford) were among the more physically attractive actors of their generation.

It also is important to recognize that the noir antihero was a substantially more passive figure than the gangster hero. While both are ultimately helpless against the determinism of society, the gangster figure at least makes a more impassioned attempt to realize the American Dream. In any event, Edward G. Robinson's involvement in both genres reflects his longstanding affiliation with a faction of American cinema that probed the darker side of masculinity and society more broadly.

Surprisingly, *Double Indemnity* did not lead to further collaborations between Robinson and Billy Wilder, a development that was due in large part to the fact that Wilder began branching out into other genres. For his next film, Edward worked with Fritz Lang, another German expatriate director. The film, *Woman in the Window* (1944), can be classified as a noir, but not as classically so as *Double Indemnity*. Where Robinson had occupied something of a supporting role in Wilder's film, Lang cast him as the protagonist. His character is Professor Wanley, a middle-aged professor whose family is on vacation. While meeting his friends for a social evening, he sees a striking portrait of a woman in a window. After studying the painting in greater detail by himself, he sees the woman and becomes acquainted with her. She is visited by her aggressive, wealthy lover while Wanley is with her, and Wanley inadvertently kills the man. This leads Wanley to become paranoid that he will be discovered as the murderer. Eventually, it is revealed that the events that have transpired were all a dream and that the woman in the painting was entirely fictitious.

Robinson in *The Woman in the Window*

As this description makes evident, there are close parallels between *The Woman in the Window* and film noir. Both involve a kind of inadequate masculinity, in which the male suffers at the hands of a threatening or seductive female. In the case of *Double Indemnity*, the insurance officer commits murder in order to satisfy the femme fatale, while in Lang's film, Robinson's attraction to the woman in the painting leads him to imagine that he has killed a man. Lang is remembered more for the German Expressionist films he made in Germany, such as *Dr. Mabuse, the Gambler* (1922) and *M* (1931) than for his Hollywood pictures, and the chiaroscuro lighting and deterministic (at least until it is shown that the professor dreamed up his crime) plotline of *The Woman in the Window* are indebted to German Expressionism but also to noir. In this sense, the movie reveals the overlap between German Expressionism and noir.

If *The Woman in the Window* can be called a noir, it is not as perfect an example of the genre as *Double Indemnity*, mainly because Robinson was markedly older than most noir protagonists. While Fred MacMurray and Robert Mitchum were relatively young, Robinson was already in his 50s. Most noir films articulate the masculine angst of men who were old enough to have fought in World War II, while Robinson was easily too old to have taken part in combat. Overall, it is perhaps more accurate to claim that *The Woman in the Window* feels more like a "Fritz Lang" film than a generic noir picture. Specifically, Tom Gunning has argued that when Robinson's character becomes fixated on the female subject of the painting, Lang continues a commitment to exploring the nature of vision in modernity, a theme which runs across his body of work. Gunning groups *The Woman in the Window* with two other Lang films, *Scarlet Street* (1945) and

The Secret Beyond the Door (1947), which he calls the "framed desire" films. In these three films, and indeed across many other Lang pictures, the vision of the male invariably leads to his downfall, either in actuality or fantasy (in the case of *The Woman in the Window*). Gunning explains, "In Lang's films the male gaze does not function as an unquestioned mode of seeing, the basic established position of spectatorship that Laura Mulvey claims it occupies in Hollywood cinema. In many ways the male voyeurs in what I will call the 'framed desire' trilogy encounter the same failure of their dreams of mastery as the master criminals/grand enunciators of the German films."

While many of Lang's male protagonists harbor aspirations of wielding great power, this is ultimately unrealized. Early in his career, Lang had directed films that featured powerful males, but the 'framed desire' films run counter to this topic. Gunning clarifies this theme further, noting, "If Lang had acknowledged the Nietzschean superman as the inspiration for his master criminals, the protagonists of the framed desire cycle recall the other end of the spectrum, Nietzsche's Last Man." These characters epitomize the pessimistic ennui of Lang, who was as deterministic as even the bleakest noir movie. In short, Lang is decorated as one of the very best directors of all time, but this is certainly not because his movies evidence any sort of narrative of uplift.

The Woman in the Window was, appropriately enough, praised highly and it led to another film between Robinson and Lang. The latter movie, *Scarlet Street*, bears much in common with the earlier one, to the point that it resonates almost as a sequel. Robinson again occupies the starring role, with Joan Bennett and Dan Duryea returning as co-stars. Robinson's standing is even lower than in *The Woman in the Window*; where he had been a professor in the prior movie, in this one he plays Christopher Cross, a cashier who has been working at the same dull job for 25 years (the film begins with him being honored for his many years of service to the company). His personal life is no more eventful, as he is married (without children) to a nagging spouse. He paints as a hobby and meets a beautiful woman (Bennett) who wrongly understands him to be a famous painter. Knowing that Cross will be unable to resist her, she ingratiates herself to him, not telling him that she already has a lover, the conman Johnny Price (Duryea).

Eventually, Cross realizes that he is being manipulated by the woman, after which he kills Bennett's character. Cross loses his job as a result, and the film ends with him in a broken state. Still, the viewer sympathizes with his character, and Andrew Spicer correctly argues that the vulnerability of Robinson's noir performances is a signature aspect of his career. He explains, "Robinson's main contribution to film noir came through very different parts that exploited his maturity and his ability, evident in his tough-guy roles, to project a thoughtful, vulnerable sensitivity."

If *The Woman in the Window* offers a bleak view of the world, the one depicted in *Scarlet Street* is even more extreme. Gone is the happy ending that marred the previous film, and the film instead emphasizes the helpless struggle of the male against the forces of fate. Gunning offers an apt description of this: "Lang de-emphasizes individual responsibility and even psychology, in favour of a fatal environment which seems not only to reflect characters' anxieties, but to trigger a series of fateful coincidences which follow from an unguarded erotic surrender, like a collapsing line of dominoes."

This account of Lang's style may seem hyperbolic, but it is no exaggeration – Lang's movies are among the darkest films ever made. *Scarlet Street* turned a fairly substantial profit, but it did not lead to any additional collaborations between Lang and Robinson, even though the actor would appear in a couple other acclaimed noirs before the end of the decade.

Robinson and Joan Bennett in *Scarlet Street*

A year after the release of *Scarlet Street*, Robinson appeared in Orson Welles' *The Stranger* (1946). By this time, Welles had, of course, already achieved a great deal. Before even turning 30, he had made *Citizen Kane* (1941), and he followed that film with *The Magnificent*

Ambersons the next year. Made by RKO Pictures, the movie is clearly a product of its time period; Robinson occupies the role of Mr. Wilson, an agent for the United Nations War Crimes Commission who is sent to small town America, where it is believed that a Nazi fugitive, Franz Kindler, is residing. The movie is essentially a prolonged cat-and-mouse game between the two, ending with a dramatic confrontation in which Kindler falls from a church and dies.

Perhaps inevitably, if viewers compare *The Stranger* with some of Welles' other, more famous cinematic achievements, they is likely to find *The Stranger* lacking. Jonathan Rosenbaum, for example, has critiqued the film for lacking the daring formal innovations of his earlier movies. That said, while it does not boast the bravura formal components that characterize Orson Welles's greatest triumphs, it is still a worthy example of noir, with an affecting portrayal of American civilian paranoia at the threat of undercover Nazis inhabiting small town America. One of the interesting aspects of the film's history is that it was an even greater commercial success than any of Welles's more decorated earlier movies had been, which can perhaps be attributed to its politically-sensitive subject matter.

Robinson and Philip Merivale in *The Stranger*

Even as Robinson progressed through his 50s, he continued to be cast in leading roles, and he starred in one film, *The Red House*, in 1947. However, his most significant film of the closing years of the decade saw him play a supporting role. The movie, *Key Largo* (1948), is widely remembered for boasting Humphrey Bogart and Lauren Bacall in the leading roles, and it was one of several movies made by Bogart and John Huston, who had worked together earlier on *The Maltese Falcon* and *The Treasure of the Sierra Madre*, the latter of which was released in 1948, earlier during the same year as *Key Largo*. Unlike most noirs, *Key Largo* was not adapted from a pulp fiction novel; instead, the source material came from a play of the same title which had enjoyed an extended run on Broadway between 1939 and 1940. Substantial changes were made to the dialogue, with the eloquent prose of the play's script replaced by rougher, more laconic dialogue that was more characteristic of noir. Bogart plays Frank McCloud, a veteran of World War II who visits a hotel in Key Largo with the intention of visiting the hotelkeeper's daughter, the widow of a friend of his who died in the war. Upon his arrival, he realizes that the hotel has been overrun by Johnny Rocco (played by Robinson), a gangster who has lost much of his power.

The movie marks a union between Bogart and Robinson, who had worked together on several occasions during the 1930s. While Robinson's character is relatively unchanged from the gangsters for whom he was still famous, seeing Bogart in *Key Largo* reveals just how much his screen persona had transformed since the previous decade. In the 1930s, Bogart had been cast mainly in villainous roles that were basically one-dimensional. What made Bogart's performances from the 1940s so memorable, meanwhile, was the way that they combined elements of heroism with a jaded, world-weary sensibility that captured the tone of America in the immediate aftermath of World War II.

Andrew Dickos has argued that *Key Largo* returns to the realm of the gangster picture but through the lens of noir, and the movie can certainly be viewed as a confrontation between the gangster film and noir, with Robinson's quintessential gangster villain defeated by the more modern noir hero played by Bogart. *Key Largo* is most commonly embraced by fans of Bogart and Bacall, as well as those of director John Huston, but the genre subtext should not be overlooked in discussions of the film.

Louisa Horton, Robinson, Chester Erskine and Burt Lancaster in a publicity photo for
All My Sons **(1948)**

Throughout the decades, Robinson had never shied away from expressing his political views, and he was one of Hollywood's leading political activists at a time when Hollywood was more overtly political than it would later become. However, Robinson's leftist leanings became problematic with the arrival of the 1950s and the emergence of the Red Scare. Three times between 1950 and 1952, he was ordered to testify before the House Un-American Activities Committee, a grueling process that entailed proving he had not donated money to the Communist Party. He also refused to name the names of anyone suspected to be Communist sympathizers, and there were certainly plenty in Hollywood.

That Robinson should be pursued by HUAC so relentlessly is surprising considering that he had never been part of the Communist Party. Ross explains the indignity of what happened to Robinson: "Studies of political activism in the movie industry during the 1940s and 1950s usually focus on the House Un-American Activities Committee (HUAC) and its attack on the ten writers, directors, and producers who refused to testify, commonly known as the Hollywood Ten…[who] were or had been Communist Party members. Therefore, it was upsetting but hardly surprising when Hollywood went after them. However, Hollywood activists were truly frightened when Red-hunters targeted those who were decidedly not Communists, particularly Eddie Robinson."

Robinson was clearly being made a scapegoat by HUAC, and even though he was exonerated on each occasion in which he testified, the events had a tangible effect on his career. He continued to act and maintained a busy schedule, but his acting opportunities grew markedly less compelling and his days as a prominent Hollywood star were clearly over.

Although none of the movies that Robinson appeared in over the first half of the decade were major successes, some of his performances remain worthy of note. In 1953, he starred in *Big Leaguer*, which holds the distinction of being the first movie directed by Robert Aldrich. The film is particularly surprising since Robinson plays a former baseball player who runs a training camp. It is somewhat shocking to see Robinson, who had never been athletic, portray a former baseball player. His performance was fine, but the movie never gained any significant attention and lost money. Faring no better was *A Bullet for Joey* (1955), a late film noir that paired Robinson with George Raft, who also had built his reputation by playing gangsters in the 1930s. By this time, Robinson was in his early 60s and Raft in his mid-50s, and the movie holds a kind of nostalgic appeal for fans of Hollywood during the 1930s.

Robinson's career rebounded somewhat when Cecil B. DeMille, himself a noted anti-Communist, took the initiative of casting Robinson in his big-budget film *The Ten Commandments* (1956). Robinson's role was as the somewhat villainous Dathan, and he was given fairly substantial screen time. In the 1950s, Hollywood gravitated closer to big-budget epics than it had at any point in its earlier history, and *The Ten Commandments* was one of the most lavish of them all. Roughly $13 million was poured into the production, and the film spans more than three-and-a-half hours (with an intermission). It is not necessarily considered a masterpiece, but its grand scope and high production values make it one of the most important films of the decade.

Robinson in *The Ten Commandments*

The 1950s also saw Robinson finally divorce Gladys Lloyd. The divorce had been a long time coming, as they had remained married for just shy of 30 years even though they were never an affectionate couple. Two years after the divorce, Robinson married Jane Bodenheimer, a much younger 38-year-old dress designer. Bodenheimer was known as Jane Adler, and she and Robinson stayed happily married for the next 15 years through the end of his life.

Robinson took a hiatus from acting for a couple of years near the end of the decade, but the 1960s saw him appear in a number of films. In 1960, he and Rod Steiger starred together in *Seven Thieves*, a bizarre movie in which Robinson was given the role of a jaded professor who joins forces with a young thief to pull off a robbery. The movie was a relatively minor affair, but it did get nominated for an Academy Award for Best Costume Design.

Another late-career highlight occurred in 1962, when Edward worked with legendary director

Vincente Minnelli on *Two Weeks in Another Town*. A reworking of Minnelli's more famous film *The Bad and the Beautiful*, *Two Weeks in Another Town* depicts the production of a Hollywood movie in Rome. Robinson plays the film's director, an aging figure who was once revered but has since seen his reputation flounder. The movie is often overlooked in assessments of Minnelli's career, but it is an interesting comment on the difficulties that aging actors have in retaining their success across different generations of Hollywood cinema.

Robinson with his son, Edward Robinson, Jr., in 1962

Over the mid-to-late 1960s, Robinson branched out into two different directions: working on Hollywood Westerns and working in Italy. During these years, Robinson starred in a series of Westerns, a genre that always had been antithetical for his screen persona. As Peter Lehman notes, "Invariably the western hero is associated with large, strong-looking men like Gary Cooper and John Wayne and the gangster genre with short men like James Cagney and Edward G. Robinson." This description, however, fits more closely with the classical Hollywood Western, but by the time Robinson began acting in Westerns, the genre was being deconstructed. An example of this can be seen in *The Outrage* (1964), a remake of Akira Kurosawa's famous Japanese film *Rashomon* (1950) set in the American West. In the movie, Robinson and three others give conflicting recollections of a murder, and as with Kurosawa's film, the movie explores the frailty of human memory.

The other significant change for Robinson during these late years of his career involved working in Italy. These films were generally over-the-top and rely on the viewer's knowledge of Robinson as an aging Hollywood star. In *Operation St. Peter's* (1967), for example, he plays a famous American criminal, while *It's Your Move* (1969) contained a similarly action-packed plot. In short, these were not the art-house Italian films of Michelangelo Antonioni or Federico Fellini but low-budget re-workings of typical Hollywood fare.

In the early 1970s, Robinson made a couple of rather minor appearances, including a small role in the Israeli-American picture *Neither by Day Nor by Night* (1972), and his last performance was in *Soylent Green* (1973), a murder mystery set in a dystopian future epoch. The film was challenging for Robinson, who by this time was suffering from bladder cancer. His health took a sharp turn for the worse, and he was barely able to make it through the film's production process. Robinson passed away due to bladder cancer on January 26, 1973, a somewhat premature conclusion to a rich and far-ranging life and career.

Given that the majority of his most famous films were in the 1930s and 1940s, it is easy to lose sight of the longevity of Edward G. Robinson's career. After all, when he began acting, the film industry had yet to even transition to sound. Edward's career owed much to the birth of sound cinema, as he only flourished after the shift to sound had been undertaken, but as one of the premier gangster actors, he played an important role in the development of the genre system in Hollywood, a system that would align him with Warner Brothers for much of his career. Moreover, Bruce Crowther has noted that Robinson was able to fluidly transition from the gangster films of the 1930s to the film noir era of the 1940s, and his involvement with both genres speaks to a central position in the violent faction of American cinema from 1930 through the early 1950s.

The longstanding success of Robinson's career also means that he made good on his parents' ambition for him to rise up the social ladder, even if one senses that Robinson could have succeeded regardless of the specific career path he chose. This was someone who did not speak a word of English when he arrived in the United States at age 10, and yet he quickly became one of the top students in his class. He was an articulate, cultured man who could think critically and develop his own opinions on worldly matters. Of course, this political consciousness also damaged his career, as evidenced by his trials before HUAC, and it is necessary to recognize that Robinson's career involved adversity. He never fully recovered from the HUAC testimonies, and there is a sense in which Robinson was not unlike a film noir hero: an intelligent, dignified victim who is nevertheless helpless in the face of social forces beyond his control.

At the same time, one of the most interesting aspects of his life and career is the discrepancy between the jumpy, quick-tempered gangsters he played in so many of his films and the intellectual strength he displayed in his personal life. To arrive at a complete picture of Edward G. Robinson, one must ultimately acknowledge both the memorable criminals he portrayed in his films and the political bravery he showcased off the movie set.

Bibliography

Crowther, Bruce. *Film Noir*. New York: Random House, 2011. E-book.

Dickos, Andrew. *Street with No Name: A History of the Classic American Film Noir*. Lexington: The University Press of Kentucky, 2002. Print.

Gansberg, Alan L. *Little Caesar: A Biography of Edward G. Robinson*. Lanham: Scarecrow Press, 2004. Print.

Germunden, Gerd. *A Foreign Affair: Billy Wilder's American Films*. New York: Berghahn Books, 2013. E-book.

Gunning, Tom. *The Films of Fritz Lang: Allegories of Vision and Modernity*. London: British Film Institute, 2000. Print.

Lehman, Peter. *Running Scared: Masculinity and the Representation of the Male Body*. Detroit: Wayne State University Press, 2007. Print.

Naremore, James. *More Than Night: Film Noir in its Contexts*. Berkeley: University of California Press, 2007. Print.

Rosenbaum, Jonathan. *Discovering Orson Welles*. Berkeley: University of California Press, 2007. Print.

Ross, Steven J. *Hollywood Left and Right: How Movie Stars Shaped American Politics*. New York: Oxford University Press, 2011. Print.

Sabin, Arthur J. *In Calmer Times: The Supreme Court and Red Monday*. Philadelphia: University of Pennsylvania Press, 1999. Print.

Shadoian, Jack. *Dreams and Dead Ends: The American Gangster Film*. New York: Oxford University Press, 2003. Print.

Spicer, Andrew. *Historical Dictionary of Film Noir*. Lanham: Scarecrow Press, 2010. Print.

Stevens, Jr., George. *Conversations with the Great Moviemakers of Hollywood's Golden Age at the American Film Institute*. New York: Random House, 2006. Print.

Szalay, Michael. *New Deal Modernism: American Literature and the Invention of the Welfare State*. Durham: Duke University Press, 2000. Print.

Warshow, Robert. "The Gangster as Tragic Hero." *Gangster Film Reader*. Eds. Alain Silve and James Ursini. Prompton Plains: Limelight Editions, 2007. 11-16. Print.

Made in the USA
San Bernardino, CA
30 May 2020